Using C&IT to Support Teaching

Communications and Information Technology (C&IT) is part of everyday life, including education. For teachers, however, keeping up to date with the various technologies that help support the learning process can be challenging.

This book meets those challenges by highlighting the benefits of C&IT in teaching and learning, and providing practical advice and real examples from a wide range of subject disciplines. Writing in a refreshingly accessible style, the author dispels common myths surrounding technology and offers pragmatic solutions that anyone can use or adapt, covering the use of:

- overhead projectors and PowerPoint;
- handouts;
- videos and slides;
- interactive whiteboards;
- electronic information resources and e-learning.

This book demonstrates that with a little thought and preparation, C&IT can provide tangible benefits in the support of traditional teaching, and will be essential reading for teachers, lecturers, staff developers and students in further and higher education.

Paul Chin is Centre Manager for the LTSN Physical Sciences Subject Centre, University of Hull.

Key Guides for Effective Teaching in Higher Education Series
Edited by Kate Exley

This indispensable series is aimed at new lecturers, postgraduate students who have teaching time, graduate teaching assistants, part-time tutors and demonstrators, as well as experienced teaching staff who may feel it's time to review their skills in teaching and learning.

Titles in this series will provide the teacher in higher education with practical, realistic guidance on the various different aspects of their teaching role, which is underpinned not only by current research in the field, but also by the extensive experience of individual authors, with a keen eye kept on the limitations and opportunities therein. By bridging a gap between academic theory and practice, all titles will provide generic guidance on teaching, learning and assessment issues which is then brought to life through the use of short illustrative examples drawn from a range of disciplines. All titles in this series will:

■ represent up-to-date thinking and incorporate the use of communication and information technologies (C&IT) where appropriate;
■ consider methods and approaches for teaching and learning when there is an increasing diversity in learning and a growth in student numbers;
■ encourage reflective practice and self-evaluation, and a means of developing the skills of teaching, learning and assessment;
■ provide links and references to further work on the topic and research evidence where appropriate.

Titles in the series will prove invaluable whether they are used for self-study or as part of a formal induction programme on teaching in higher education, and will also be of relevance to teaching staff working in further education settings.

Other titles in this series:

Assessing Students' Written Work
– Catherine Haines
Giving a Lecture: From Presenting to Teaching
– Kate Exley and Reg Dennick
Small Group Teaching
– Kate Exley and Reg Dennick

Using C&IT to Support Teaching

Paul Chin

RoutledgeFalmer
Taylor & Francis Group

LONDON AND NEW YORK

First published 2004
by RoutledgeFalmer
11 New Fetter Lane, London EC4P 4EE

Simultaneously published in the USA and Canada
by RoutledgeFalmer
29 West 35th Street, New York, NY 10001

RoutledgeFalmer is an imprint of the Taylor & Francis Group

Typeset in Perpetua and Bell Gothic by
Florence Production Ltd, Stoodleigh, Devon
Printed and bound in Great Britain by
Biddles Ltd, King's Lynn, Norfolk

Key Guides for Effective Teaching in Higher Education web resource

The Key Guides for Effective Teaching in Higher Education Series provides guidance and advice for those looking to improve their teaching and learning. It is accompanied by a useful website which features brand new supplementary material, including How Students Learn, a guide written by Professor George Brown which provides outlines and commentaries on theories of learning and their implications for teaching practice.

Visit the website at: http://www.routledgefalmer.com/series/KGETHE

The RoutledgeFalmer website also features a wide range of books for lecturers and higher education professionals

British Library Cataloguing in Publication Data
A catalogue record for this book is available from the British Library

Library of Congress Cataloging in Publication Data
Chin, Paul, 1968–
     Using C&IT to support teaching / Paul Chin.
         p. cm. – (Effective teaching in higher education)
     Includes bibliographical references and index.
         1. Education, Higher – Effect of technological innovations on.
     2. College teaching – Computer network resources.   3. Information
     technology.   I. Title: Using communications and information technology
     to support teaching.   II. Title.   III. Series.
     LB2395.7.C45 2004
     378.1′2′0285 – dc22 2003019840

ISBN 0–415–30714–7 (hbk)
ISBN 0–415–30715–5 (pbk)

This book is dedicated to my wife, Andrea,
for her patience with me over the last year and
hopefully for many years to come!

Contents

Series preface

This series of books grew out of discussions with new lecturers and part-time teachers in universities and colleges who were keen to develop their teaching skills. However, experienced colleagues may also enjoy and find merit in the books, particularly the discussions about current issues that are impacting on teaching and learning in further and higher education (e.g. widening participation, disability legislation and the integration of C&IT in teaching).

New lecturers may be required by their institutions to take part in teaching development programmes. This frequently involves attending workshops, investigating teaching through mini projects and reflecting on their practice. Many teaching programmes ask participants to develop their own teaching portfolios and to provide evidence of their developing skills and understanding. Scholarship of teaching is usually an important aspect of the teaching portfolio. New teachers can be asked to consider their own approach to teaching in relation to the wider literature, research findings and theory of teaching and learning. However, when people are beginning their teaching careers, a much more pressing need may be to design and deliver an effective teaching session for tomorrow. Hence the intention of this series is to provide a complementary mix of very practical teaching tips and guidance, together with a strong basis and clear rationale for their use.

In many institutions the numbers of part-time and occasional teachers actually outnumber the full-time staff. Yet the provision of formal training and development for part-time teachers is more sporadic and variable across the sector. As a result, this diverse group of educators can feel isolated and left out of the updating and support offered to their full-time counterparts. Never have there been so many part-time teachers involved in the design and delivery of courses, the support and guidance of students, and the monitoring and assessment of learning. The group also includes the thousands of postgraduate students who work as laboratory demonstrators, problem-class tutors, project supervisors and class teachers. It includes clinicians, lawyers and professionals who contribute their specialist knowledge and skills to enrich the learning experience for many vocational and professional course students. And it includes the many hourly-paid and jobbing tutors who have helped full-time staff to cope with the expansion and diversification of further and higher education.

Universities sometimes struggle to know how many part-time staff they employ to teach and, as a group, occasional teachers are notoriously difficult to contact systematically through university and college communication systems. Part-time and occasional teachers often have other roles and responsibilities, and teaching is a small but important part of what they do day to day. Many part-time tutors would not expect to undertake the full range of teaching activities of full-time staff, but may well do lots of tutoring or lots of class teaching and yet never lecture or supervise (or vice versa). So the series provides short practical books that focus squarely on different teaching roles and activities. The first four books published are:

Small Group Teaching
Giving a Lecture: From Presenting to Teaching
Assessing Students' Written Work
Using C&IT to Support Teaching

The books are all very practical with detailed discussion of teaching techniques and methods, though still based on educational theory and research findings. Articles are referenced, further readings and related web sites are given, and workers in the field are quoted and acknowledged. To this end Dr George Brown has been commissioned to produce an accompanying web-based guide on student learning which can be freely accessed by readers. The guide provides a substantial foundation for the teaching and assessment practices discussed and recommended in the texts. The link to this guide is given at the end of Chapter 1.

There is much enthusiasm and support here too for the excellent work currently being carried out by the Learning and Teaching Support networks within discipline groupings (indeed, individual LTSN centres are suggested as sources of further information throughout these volumes). The need to provide part-time tutors with realistic connections with their own disciplines is keenly felt by all the authors in the series and 'how it might work in your department' examples are given at the end of many of the activity-based chapters. However, there is without doubt some merit in sharing teaching developments across the boundaries of discipline, culture and country, as many of the problems in the tertiary education sector are themselves widely shared.

UNDERLYING THEMES

The use of Communications and Information Technology (C&IT) to enrich student learning and to help manage the workload of teachers is a recurrent theme in the series. I acknowledge that not all teachers may yet have access to state-of-the-art teaching resources and facilities. However, the use of virtual learning environments, e-learning provision and audio-visual presentation media is becoming increasingly widespread in universities.

The books also acknowledge and try to help new teachers respond to the growing and changing nature of the student population. Students with non-traditional educational backgrounds, international students and students who have disabilities or special needs are encouraged through the government's widening participation agenda to take part in further and higher education. The books seek to advise teachers on current legislative requirements and offer guidance on recommended good practice in teaching diverse groups of students.

These were our goals, and I and my co-authors sincerely hope these volumes prove to be a helpful resource for colleagues, both new and experienced, in further and higher education.

Kate Exley
July 2003

Acknowledgements

I would like to acknowledge the following people for offering their time and patience to help me in the preparation of this book. They were willing to provide advice and feedback at short notice and without reservation. So thank you to David Pennie, Richard Middleton and Steve Walker.

I would also like to extend my immense gratitude to Alistair Anderson, Katy Barnett, Roger Gladwin and Tina Overton who helped me more times than I care to remember.

Finally, I would like to give a special mention to my close friend, Mark Bell, who designed and produced all the artwork contained in this book. Your ability to turn vague ideas into clever and artistic cartoons is amazing.

Introduction

Perhaps one of the biggest problems for teachers when considering the adoption of Communications and Information Technology (C&IT) is the confidence and self-belief to use the technology available to students. Many teachers may be comfortable using a computer at their desk or at home to prepare work, email people and use the Web, but recoil at the idea of applying these skills to their teaching.

The sceptics or technophobes are always the first to point out the potential pitfalls of attempting to use C&IT to support teaching: you need to be a technical wizard; or the technology is unreliable; or the benefits are not worth the effort or cost. Although these can be valid arguments, they can also often be weak excuses for not engaging in modern teaching practices and not using equipment widely available in most teaching institutions.

This book does not attempt to pretend that the use of C&IT is always easy and straightforward. Indeed, the author would be the first to agree with the more weary that when things go wrong, it can be very frustrating and annoying. However, the author also strongly feels that a 'Luddite' attitude is not a valid reason for ignoring the potential benefits that C&IT has to offer and hopes to dispel some of the negative myths about the shortcomings of C&IT.

The aim of this book, therefore, is to take a pragmatic approach to the ways in which C&IT can be used to support teaching, backed up by evidence of good practice and known research. Potential pitfalls of using technology in particular instances are readily highlighted, but the book also provides practical advice on how to avoid such problems, or how to react when things do go wrong.

There are also reasons other than just teacher attitude that need to be considered for the adoption of C&IT. The most obvious one is simply that technology invades every aspect of our society and is difficult to ignore. Therefore, our students are used to using technology in their everyday lives; it is also commonly used at primary and secondary level education, so students *expect* to use it. For example, people can now access video and the Web via mobile telephones, so why not also in the classroom?

Another knock-on effect of technology in society is that employers also expect our graduating students to have C&IT experience to cope with the modern working environment. Therefore, students should not be denied the chance to use C&IT when studying.

In terms of benefits for teachers, C&IT is simply a form of technology that, by definition, should automate work and hence make life easier for us all. C&IT is not intended to be a replacement for face-to-face teaching but an aid to existing teaching methods. As with anything new there is always a learning curve, but hopefully this book will smooth that curve and provide practical advice on how to use C&IT in an effective and efficient manner that will ultimately benefit both teachers and students.

Chapter 1

Why not just use chalk?

Why not just use chalk? This may seem an obvious question; after all, most teaching has been done this way for several hundred years. Teachers are familiar with using chalk to convey information on the blackboard, which the students can then copy. There are a number of benefits of teaching this way as teachers are able to stand in front of a class and chat informally to their students. The flow of information can be dynamic as teachers are able to chalk ideas onto the blackboard and discuss the content as they proceed. Equally, students can also ask questions to which the teachers can respond, giving immediate feedback.

While this is the normal delivery method for teaching, and will continue to be so, there are inherent problems with this method of teaching. Lectures came about partly because teachers were the only people with access to 'textbooks', but these days all students can have access to the same information as their teachers. In addition, large student numbers reduce the ability to interact, putting pressure on teachers to deliver content in the brief time available, which leaves little time for questions.

These factors often combine to reduce lectures to monologues where teachers talk at their students for fifty minutes or so. Some teachers are naturally self-confident, good orators and comfortable with this approach, but not all teachers are capable of giving dynamic public performances – which is no reflection on their ability to teach. However, what is the point of lectures if teachers simply talk at the class or read their notes for the entire period?

If we consider lectures from the students' point of view, no matter how interesting the subject or topic may be, attention spans always wane after about fifteen to twenty minutes. Students do not all learn the same way either and teachers will inevitably teach in their own preferred style. Therefore, lectures can greatly benefit from a change of format and the introduction of C&IT can add great value to the teaching and learning experience. If we could re-invent teaching again, would we start with the lecture?

THE LEARNING PROCESS

In order to appreciate how C&IT can enhance teaching and learning it is important to discuss the process of learning and how technology can support that process. By considering how we, the teachers learn, as well as how students learn, it is possible to design and embed C&IT into the curriculum with maximum effect. A lot of research has been undertaken over the decades on the subject of learning and several authors have become well recognised, such as Piaget, Vygotsky and Bloom (who developed Bloom's taxonomy of learning). Although these researchers have become well known for their work on learning, much of their research is too complex for discussion within the context of this book.

However, two strands of research do provide a pragmatic approach to the learning process: those of David Kolb (1984) and Peter Honey and Alan Mumford (1986). Kolb discussed how people learn through experience and devised an experiential learning cycle, as shown in Figure 1.1. This model was revised by Honey and Mumford in 1986, who proposed four basic learning styles. They also devised a questionnaire which helps people identify their own preferred learning style. By being aware of our preferred style of learning and those of our students, we are in a better position to help students learn in a way that best suits them. The four learning styles Honey and Mumford defined are:

- **activist** – people who take a hands-on approach to problems and tasks;
- **theorist** – people who postulate ideas based on analysis and objectivity;
- **pragmatist** – practical people who apply new ideas immediately;
- **reflector** – thoughtful people who consider all possibilities before taking action.

So, what does all this mean in terms of teaching and learning? If we consider Kolb's learning cycle, it shows that people learn from concrete experience, which they then reflect on. This information or knowledge

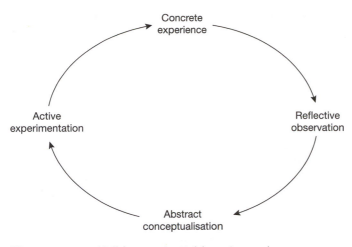

Concrete
experience

Reflective
observation

Active
experimentation

Abstract
conceptualisation

FIGURE 1.1 Kolb's experiential learning cycle

must then be conceptualised or 'internalised' and then backed up by active experimentation. Therefore, students learn by: taking in information; reflecting on it; digesting the information; and then experimenting in various ways to back up what they have learnt.

However, since people learn in different ways, they will follow this cycle according to their own preferences. For example, activists will approach a problem head-on and test various ideas to see what works or what does not. Based on the outcomes and their observations, they will then reflect before internalising the information as knowledge, i.e. they will have learnt from their experience. For more information about student learning, refer to the web-based guide that accompanies this series, cited at the end of this chapter.

USING C&IT TO SUPPORT THE LEARNING PROCESS

Stephen Alessi and Stanley Trollip (2001) discuss the application of technology to the process of learning and highlight four general learning activities that have been shown to be successful through research, namely:

- presenting information;
- guiding the learner;
- practising;
- assessing learning.

3

These four activities reflect Kolb's learning cycle, whereby assessment is an external process to help reinforce a student's conceptualisation of a topic. There are a number of ways that teachers can engage in these four activities:

- lectures;
- tutorials;
- drill and practice exercises;
- group exercises (role play, games, simulations etc.);
- open-ended tasks (project work, case studies etc.).

C&IT can supplement these activities using a number of different methods:

- online tutorials etc.;
- simulations;
- knowledge reinforcement exercises;
- open-ended learning environments;
- computer-assisted assessment.

Technology can be employed to support each or all of these activities. It can deliver content that students can use in much the same way as content is delivered through a formal lecture. It can provide guidance on topics, through carefully crafted exercises which can be reinforced by practice activities. Finally, technology can be used to assess student learning through formative and summative testing. However, C&IT alone does not cover all activities and the technology itself is not a substitute for face-to-face teaching but acts as an enhancement to it. Therefore, the appropriate use of C&IT, tied in with face-to-face teaching and support, can improve the learning process for students and bring a number of benefits for teachers.

At a fundamental level of teaching support, C&IT can help you as a teacher to enhance lectures in a classroom setting:

- confidence with your students can be improved;
- improved eye contact can be developed when students switch between the technology and yourself;
- a better rapport can be established with the students paying more attention when you are speaking;
- points can be better illustrated with visually appealing examples;

■ absentees can benefit greatly as the resources are accessible after the class.

THE DEVELOPMENT OF C&IT

Technology has been used to support teaching and learning since the 1960s when overhead projectors allowed teachers to project their work to larger audiences in a more visually stimulating format. The use of video in the classroom also provided extra stimulation and photocopiers (or Xerox machines as they used to be known) allowed content to be quickly reproduced and distributed.

However, over the last twenty years or so C&IT has developed at such a fantastic rate that now there are a huge number of electronic tools available to support students. Many of the commonly available types of technology are discussed in this book, but the continuing development of technology will mean that these tools will soon be more compact, portable, increasingly wireless and cheaper.

WHY SHOULD I USE TECHNOLOGY?

It is true that the use of technology requires initial investments of time and effort, but these are short-term endeavours for long-term gains. Technology offers a number of advantages:

■ it saves time;
■ it enhances learning;
■ it accommodates more students;
■ it's cheaper;
■ it's innovative;
■ it's easy to use;
■ students find it interesting.

A major reason for using C&IT, however, is because the students expect it.

A cautionary note about adopting C&IT

Although this book takes a pragmatic approach to the use of C&IT in teaching and learning, the advantages listed above have potential pitfalls. Initially, adopting C&IT will take longer than more traditional methods of teaching as it will take time to plan and prepare electronic resources. However, the potential long-term benefits will eventually lead to savings in time.

There is an ongoing argument about whether technology can enhance the learning process but, if used appropriately, it can be at least as valid as some face-to-face teaching methods, for example, when considering information delivery and communication. Cost savings may be longer term after initial investments in hardware, software and possible training costs have been assessed.

When considering how innovative C&IT can be, it is not necessarily a case of how advanced the technology is. What may be new technology to one teacher may be standard to another. Therefore, innovation with technology comes from the way it is used – and this is what leads to ease of use and how interesting it can make learning for the students. Using C&IT to support teaching and learning is only advantageous if it is planned and delivered with an appropriate use in mind.

ACCESSIBILITY AND SENDA

In 1995 the Disability Discrimination Act (DDA) was introduced in the UK to prevent discrimination against disabled people. In September 2002 this was extended to post-sixteen education with the Special Educational Needs and Disability Act (SENDA). Although SENDA is separate legislation, it is actually just part four of the DDA. What this means is that tertiary education must now ensure that it actively takes steps to avoid discriminating against disabled students.

For example, the provision of resources for blind students is directly relevant to the SENDA leglislation. Institutions do not have to have, for example, sets of resources available in Braille *just in case* a prospective blind student applies to do a course. However, the institution must ensure that it has the means to produce a set of Braille resources if required. This is an important point. The issue is not so much that institutions have to physically provide a full range of measures and provision for *potential* disabled applicants, but that they must have in place the *capability* to cater for disabled students should they apply. In the legislation this is referred to as making 'reasonable adjustments'.

One of the potential benefits of using C&IT to support teaching and learning is that it offers technological ways of supporting disabled students in their studies. This would mean that existing teaching methods might not require much adaptation to cater for the support of disabled students. Staying with the example of blind students, there are now software programs that can reproduce text on a computer screen as audio output. One example is a program called Jaws that 'reads' the text to the listener.

There is a wide range of computer technologies for supporting disabled students, too many to discuss in detail for the context of this book. However, at relevant points in different chapters reference is made to the technology and how it can be of specific help to disabled students. It does not mean that technology is only applicable for certain aspects of support. We should always bear in mind provision for disabled students and remember that SENDA is *legislation*, not a suggestion. Using C&IT, however, can overcome many of the potential barriers to support for disabled students. There are several national bodies that can offer support and advice on this topic.

Using C&IT in tertiary education

Computer technology is now commonly used at all levels of education, so by the time that students reach further and higher education, they have already experienced C&IT in the classroom. For example, teachers at primary and secondary level now commonly use interactive whiteboards in class and students are familiar with using the Web to search for information. Even mature students, for example, are familiar with technology through the media. They know about the Web and many use email. They may even use C&IT in their everyday lives for such services as online banking or shopping.

Students who enter further and higher education will automatically assume that teachers and lecturers will also be using this technology. Therefore, students will be surprised if their teachers do not use technology and will wonder why they are shown outdated modes of doing things when they know that more advanced technological alternatives exist.

I do not intend to embarrass people into using technology, especially for the wrong reasons, but it is a valid point to make that some students will be perplexed by teachers who avoid technology altogether. Teachers are supposed to teach new materials and be more knowledgeable than the students, but their integrity will be questioned by some if they understand little about the various technologies that pervade society today.

C&IT has a lot to offer teaching and learning, and the benefits for both teachers and students are clear. Although this book is aimed at demonstrating some of the common uses of technology and provides numerous examples across the disciplines, it also attempts to take a pragmatic approach. In this sense, the most important point I would make is to be clear about your reason for using technology in the first place. Trying to use, and failing with, technology in front of students can be just as damaging as not using it at all.

Just as important as knowing how to use technology (after all we may know how to turn a video player on) is how to use it *appropriately* for teaching purposes. Students will quickly become disillusioned by the technology and the teachers if there is no clear purpose for using technology. Playing a video clip may provide variety to a class, but if the teacher doesn't explain how the students should use the content, it adds nothing to the learning process.

One final point to be made about using C&IT to support teaching and learning is that this book is not necessarily designed to be a technical 'how to' book. Chapter 2 discusses the issue of developing technical skills and where to seek help, but the rest of the book is aimed at introducing the various technologies and providing examples. The majority of examples are real ones already being used in education and have been shown to work, although others are suggestions which demonstrate good use of the technology. The reason for providing context-based examples is to provide practical ideas and suggestions which may be used or adapted to suit individual preferences.

FURTHER READING

Curzon, Leslie (1990) *Teaching in Further Education: An Outline of Principles and Practice* (Chapter 12, 'Taxonomies of Learning Objectives'), 4th edn, London: Cassell.

Fry, Heather, Ketteridge, Steve and Marshall, Stephanie (1999) *A Handbook for Teaching and Learning in Higher Education*, London: Kogan Page.

Internet Teaching, available online at http://www.oucs.ox.ac.uk/ltg/projects/jtap/reports/teaching/basic.html (accessed 04/08/03).

Key Guides for Effective Teaching in Higher Education. A Web-based resource on student learning to support this series, http://www.routledgefalmer.com/series/KGETHE.

Maier, Pat and Warren, Adam (2002) *Integrating Technology in Teaching and Learning: A Practical Guide for Educators*, London: Kogan Page.

Chapter 2

Preparing the students

In the developed world we live in today, it is expected that people should have a basic level of numeracy and literacy, but it is also becoming increasingly expected that people should have a basic level of IT literacy too. For example, in everyday life:

- people use technology to use ATM cash machines;
- programming the video is a stereotyped example of technology in the home; and
- the advent of digital services through the television also means that more people than ever are now able to use the Web and various other computer services such as email.

Most employers would expect employees (graduate or otherwise) to have at least some basic C&IT skills. Office work, for example, is dominated by the use of computers and even areas such as the service industry use cash registers which require the user to have a reasonable understanding of computerised automation. This, inevitably, has an effect on people's attitudes to technology that has to be taken into account when using C&IT to support education.

ATTITUDES TO C&IT SKILLS

The teacher perspective

Since we now expect students to have basic C&IT skills, such as word processing, it is not unreasonable to expect teachers to have the same level of competence. Indeed, most teachers have no problem using a word processor to type their lecture notes or using email. However, when it comes to applying these skills to more specifically tailored uses, many can experience a lack of confidence in their own ability. 'Typing lecture notes is one thing, but producing fully interactive learning resources is another' is a common response.

About ten to fifteen years ago this was certainly true because staff would have needed quite considerable C&IT skills or formal programming expertise to be able to develop electronic teaching and learning resources. However, with the rapid development of technology since then, it is possible to produce these electronic resources quite easily with little more than basic word processing skills.

Teachers are becoming more comfortable with the use of technology, and, for example, are able to produce quite interesting web resources. There are many software tools available that make it easy to produce web pages without any special programming skills. Some of these tools are called web authoring tools whereby the teacher types in the content and the software converts it into a web page. Examples of these tools include Microsoft FrontPage, Adobe GoLive and Macromedia Dreamweaver. Even standard word processors can automatically convert documents into web pages.

An additional factor that has changed teacher attitudes to the use of C&IT is the level of support and training available. Many institutions now have dedicated training teams that provide specific training tailored to the needs of the individual on a wide range of computer technologies, ranging from word processing and spreadsheet skills to web design and video editing training. There is also an increasing number of external units that provide training. One example is the Netskills training unit that was initiated by the JISC (Joint Information Systems Committee) and is now run by Newcastle University.

Therefore, by and large, teachers generally have the necessary skills and should be relatively comfortable with the prospect of using C&IT to support the learning process. Even if they lack confidence with the use of C&IT, they usually have a means of support and training to help them develop these core skills.

The issue of scepticism from some teachers concerning the use of C&IT is a serious one: it is important that students are not denied access to valuable electronic resources because of individual prejudice. However, from the teacher's point of view, developing such skills can be daunting and time consuming to say the least. It is important therefore to realise that technology has developed in ways that enable the user, i.e. the teacher, to produce quite complex and interactive resources without the need to be a specialist programmer.

The student perspective

In order to consider student attitudes to the use of C&IT skills in further and higher education, we must first consider the backgrounds of these students. Although the common view is that most students who enter tertiary education are young 18–20 year olds, we must also consider mature students, who are increasing in numbers each year, especially due to widening participation initiatives.

C&IT is increasingly being used at primary and secondary level, with the result that students are now entering tertiary education having experienced technology-supported teaching and learning as the norm. Mature students, on the other hand, may be returning to education after a break, so not only are they unfamiliar with the education system, but they may also have had very little direct contact with the use of technology. The result is that teachers face a mix of students with, potentially, a wide variety of computer skills.

There are two further issues with this mix of students. The first is the issue of dealing with students who lack C&IT skills and who may be afraid of the technology if they feel 'left behind' with developments. These students are referred to as experiencing 'technophobia' and feel they will never be able to develop these skills. The second issue is an opposite effect, where students have a grasp of C&IT but overestimate their own skills, or at least overestimate the level of skills they have when compared to those expected in tertiary education and by employers.

A cautionary note about C&IT skills

One of the reasons that teachers and subsequently students have a negative experience with using C&IT is the assumptions made about the level of C&IT skills that students have. If teachers adopt computer technology to support their teaching, they often spend time familiarising themselves with it and will be fully conversant by the time they expose the students to the technology.

However, for the reasons stated earlier, students may not have the previous experience required to use the technology, so it is important that teachers are aware of this. Expecting students to learn with the aid of technology can cause a number of problems if the students are not prepared and have not been trained to use it.

The first potential problem is that the students will simply not use the technology to access the resources on offer. If the content is tied to some sort of assessment, this automatically puts such students at a disadvantage. The next problem is that if students are unsuccessful in using the technology, then it will cause confusion and result in extra demands on the teachers' time should they have to provide additional support. This also means that more time is spent focusing on the technology itself and not the content – which should be the primary reason for using technology.

Another issue is being aware of student subject backgrounds as, historically, science-oriented students tend to be more technologically experienced than, say, humanities students. Although this is a generalisation, the point is that teachers should be aware of the IT literacy of their students and should build in capacity to support students in the use of C&IT in the classroom.

Gauging student C&IT literacy

In order for students to use C&IT in the classroom, it is important to gauge the level of skills competence they initially have. The most obvious assessment of skills is to check student experience based on previous courses or qualifications. This can be undertaken by asking all students to complete a questionnaire to gauge their level of IT literacy. Although this can give you a quick idea of the sorts of skills the students claim to have, there is a danger of being slightly misled by the responses. Some students will over- or underestimate the level of skills they have in relation to what is expected at tertiary level education.

Another way of gauging student IT literacy is to give them a standard C&IT skills test to assess their competence. Although this sort of test takes time to administer, it is a very useful activity which can overcome many future problems. The test can be a simple review of some of the core skills required. The test helps students to confirm the skills they have or identifies areas where they need to focus on further training.

In the case of students who feel they have relevant previous experience, it helps to clarify whether their skills match with what is expected. It is at this stage that their skills are confirmed or they can be shown to be missing some. This can be very useful since many students become complacent about engaging with C&IT unless it is made clear to them which skills are required. For students with little or no previous experience, the test helps to identify key skills which they may be lacking and which they can work towards developing.

HOW DO WE PREPARE THE STUDENTS?

There are several ways to prepare students for using C&IT to support the learning process. The most important aspect is to provide students with the necessary C&IT skills which they can then apply to whatever computer technology is presented to them. Students must be made aware that they are not being taught to use particular software programs, but that they are being given the skills which they can apply to equivalent software programs. That C&IT skills are transferable skills must therefore be stressed to the students. All too often students remark 'I can use Microsoft Word' when they should understand that they can use word processing software. They need to appreciate that if presented with a different word processing package, Corel WordPerfect for example, their skills would be equally applicable.

Demonstrations

Perhaps the apparently easiest approach for you as a teacher to take with your students is to demonstrate the technology step by step in the classroom. Although this approach has a number of benefits, more often than not the students only feel they are learning how to use one particular software tool rather than developing more general C&IT skills. Unless adequate time is allowed to demonstrate the software and reinforce the transferability of the skills being taught, this approach should generally be reserved for demonstrating specialised software.

One example of this is something as simple as saving a file on a PC (as opposed to a Macintosh computer). It is straightforward to show students how to save a file from within a particular software program, but they will not understand about file extensions, a three-letter addition to the file name which identifies the type of file. This is an important skill since many students have problems locating and opening files with the correct software if they do not understand about file extensions.

Ad hoc support

Another way of preparing the students is to provide extracurricular support to develop their C&IT skills. This support may come in a number of guises. The first is the offer of ad hoc training sessions, possibly with you or your colleagues, or even with experienced students such as research students who have the necessary skills. Some institutions even make ex-gratia payments to higher level or experienced students to provide help to other students.

Depending on the type and size of institution, you may have a dedicated computer services unit. Quite often this unit is able to provide a student support desk where students can call in to ask for specific help. With this sort of service there is always the risk of high demand, which can limit the amount of help available at any one time. To counter this, many computer services units also provide help leaflets that cover many of the basic C&IT issues.

Study support services

In addition to ad hoc support there are also a number of dedicated central services that some institutions provide specifically for C&IT support. This can include central study support services units which sometimes provide structured student classes for developing C&IT skills over and above any ad hoc support they provide. Study support services usually provide additional services such as mathematics support, essay writing and other study skills advice.

The services are usually provided on a drop-in basis and are often hosted in a library, which should have easy accessibility and central location. The unit would be manned by a range of full- and part-time specialist tutors. Students can request extended meetings through an appointment system, which ensures that individuals or groups of students can get specific help based on their own needs.

Alongside the study service units many institutions provide a range of C&IT training booklets. Booklets of this nature are mainly self-directed so that students can work on them individually and in their own time. The booklets may be free of charge, charged at cost price or perhaps subsidised through the department or institution.

Formal C&IT courses

The most detailed but most beneficial way to ensure that students gain the necessary C&IT skills is to provide formal courses. This ensures that students are fully prepared for engaging with technology-supported teaching and learning. There are several ways to offer these courses: as core classes which all students have to attend; as optional classes depending on student choice; or a mixture of both. The last option would involve an assessment of students' skills and any who did not attain a basic level of understanding would be required to undertake the course.

A potential problem with structured C&IT courses, however, is that they have a tendency to be generic. Students studying a subject-based course who then follow a generic IT course often have difficulty relating the skills to what they are studying. A classic example is when students are taught how to use spreadsheets. Regardless of the subject, many spreadsheet exercises tend to be based around fictitious sales figures which have no bearing on the subject whatsoever. As a result, many students find it difficult to relate their computing skills to their subject discipline and switch off from the learning process.

If students are taught C&IT skills in context, they are able to take an interest in the course, knowing that the skills have real applications. Many students have often been slightly confused by the presence of an IT module in their course when they are studying languages, sociology or even English. Putting C&IT skills into context, for example in a history course, would be to deliver the same spreadsheet skills using real historical data, such as census information.

One exception to this approach is the European Computer Driving Licence (ECDL). This qualification is recognised throughout the European Community and is administered in the UK through the British Computer Society. Although this is a generic course it ensures that anyone who completes the qualification has attained a proficient standard of C&IT skills. The qualification is recognised by different European countries and employers.

The ECDL is administered by a local test centre, which may be an accredited unit within your own institution. Although a generic course, the incentive for students to undertake the ECDL is that it leads to a qualification in its own right. Students can then use this as direct evidence of IT proficiency which is a valuable transferable skill.

What next after basic training?

It is unlikely that any one institution is able to offer the full range of training and courses listed in this chapter. Sometimes providing C&IT training is a matter of compromise, perhaps with the use of independent study books backed up by class demonstrations and tutorials.

However, it is vitally important that students are given this training since you, as the teacher, cannot expect students to use technology as part of their studies if they lack basic C&IT skills. A common mistake that some teachers make is to assume students have or will attain these skills independently and without support.

Having made provision to gauge the level of skills among your students and also provided the means to bring everyone up to a common level of proficiency, the students will be well prepared to work with a range of computer technologies. Subsequently, it will only take minimal effort to familiarise students with the variety of computer technologies available for supporting teaching and learning.

📖 FURTHER READING

Cottrell, Stella (2001) *Teaching Study Skills and Supporting Learning*, Basingstoke: Palgrave.

Forsyth, Ian (1998) *Teaching and Learning Materials and the Internet*, London: Kogan Page.

Laurillard, Diana (2002) *Rethinking University Teaching: A Framework for the Effective Use of Learning Technologies*, 2nd edn, London: RoutledgeFalmer.

Race, Phil (1993) *Never Mind the Teaching – Feel the Learning*, SEDA Paper 80, Birmingham: Staff and Educational Development Association Publications.

Chapter 3

Overhead projectors and PowerPoint

ADVANTAGES OF USING THE OVERHEAD PROJECTOR

The overhead projector (OHP) is probably the most common presentation tool available to a teacher in the classroom or lecture theatre. It is therefore a very good starting point for most people when preparing and using learning resources. However, due to its physical ease of use (all you need do is switch the OHP on), it is also very easy to miss its real potential as a valuable teaching tool.

With a little thought an OHP can be a very effective and flexible aid to teaching, helping to convey important visual messages and concepts to students. It is possible to prepare the overhead transparencies (also commonly referred to as acetates) which are projected by OHPs prior to the class. This means that more time can be spent discussing issues in class rather than simply delivering notes.

One of the other main advantages of using an OHP is the ability to engage with the students. When using a chalk/whiteboard the teacher has to turn away from the students, thus momentarily losing a connection with them and their train of thought as they focus on you while you write. By using an OHP your notes are already available and you are able to maintain contact with the students at all times since you are still facing them.

By maintaining eye contact with your students you can engage with their body language more, and they yours. For example, if you are displaying some notes or an image, it is possible to gauge student reaction and use this to explore the topic more. Since you are facing the students they can also relate to you and, depending on your position, you can promote a more informal atmosphere. So if you sit by the OHP,

It was clear Dr Bell didn't know how to use the OHP

say, it gives more of an impression of being part of the group and reduces the formality of teaching compared with standing or sitting behind a desk.

Some advantages of using an overhead projector include:

- ease of use;
- better prepared notes;
- conveys information using visual prompts;
- saves time having to write notes during class;
- you can interact with students more.

PREPARATION OF ACETATES

Although there may appear to be a lot to think about when using an OHP, the most important aspect is the content that you will be showing. Many people make the fundamental mistake of producing content for display on an acetate as if they were handouts or detailed notes. An overhead transparency should be used to highlight key items that are a reference point for the lecture or discussion and not to transmit the main content. Therefore, there are some key guidelines that should be followed when producing acetates.

Purpose

When using acetates, they should have a clear purpose, such as providing an aid to note taking. Remember that this means an *aid* to note taking and not the *core* function of the lecture. This means that students should be able to digest what is being presented and not simply be expected to write things down without being given a chance to understand the material. Acetates can also be used to illustrate a point, such as examples of a concept or idea being discussed. Another purpose for using acetates is that they can offer a variation in the mode of presentation. Rather than talk continuously to the students, the use of acetates at appropriate points can help maintain their attention and interest. The reverse is also true however, since a lecture consisting of one acetate after another can be just as boring.

Legibility

Although printing notes and other materials onto acetates will automatically make the content more legible than handwritten notes, there are also other factors to consider for producing a well-presented acetate. In order to enable the students to read your notes, the minimum font size you should use on an acetate should be 16 to 18 point; otherwise it will be too difficult to read. If you feel you need to reduce font size to fit the required amount of text onto one acetate, then you almost certainly have too much content on one sheet to start with. You should therefore just split the content onto separate sheets. To check visibility of an acetate you should walk to the back of the room and determine how legible the text is from there.

Visual appeal

Using acetates should help maintain student interest and therefore it makes sense to ensure the content is visually appealing. This can be done in a number of ways using images and colours. Images can help visualise a point, but even the occasional use of clip art can improve the visual appeal of text (Figure 3.1). Be careful, however, not to get carried away with the use of clip art as it can become too distracting for the student. If you intend to use colour, this can also improve visual appeal, e.g. the use of coloured text to highlight certain points, but be aware that some colours are difficult to read. Highlighting a word

19

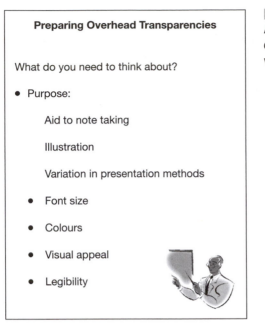

Preparing Overhead Transparencies

What do you need to think about?

- Purpose:

    Aid to note taking

    Illustration

    Variation in presentation methods

- Font size

- Colours

- Visual appeal

- Legibility

■ **FIGURE 3.1**
Acetate with simple clip art to improve visual appeal

or phrase in red, say, may make it stand out, but colour-blind students will not be able to read it. About five to eight per cent of the male population and one to two per cent of the female population are colour blind. Therefore, while the use of colour can help, the choice of colour and its use should be appropriate for the purpose.

SETTING UP AN OHP

There is a plethora of OHPs available on the market today and, indeed, you are likely to meet several different types even in your own department or institution. Regardless of variety, an OHP still only has one basic function: to project light onto a display area for viewing. Therefore while it is impossible to describe in detail how to operate different makes of OHP, each offers several basic functions. Figure 3.2 shows a typical overhead projector.

Light source

The most important function of an OHP is its light source, which is produced by an electric bulb. Bulbs can last for several months or several

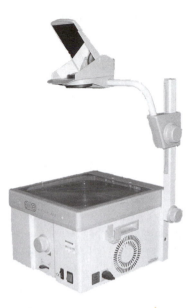

FIGURE 3.2 Overhead projector

years, depending on their level of use, and are usually either 250 W or
400 W. Many OHPs have a spare bulb in case the primary bulb blows
and can usually be changed by a handle or switch that rotates the new
bulb into position. However, you should always be prepared just in case
there is no spare. For example, do you know where spare bulbs are
stored and how to change it or do you need to contact a porter for
help?

Adjusting the screen focus

In most cases, the focus is set by adjusting the height of the projector lens.
This can be adjusted until a crisp, sharp image is produced on the display
area, which may be a projector screen or other non-reflective white surface. In addition, the size of the display produced is also dependent on
the distance of the OHP from the display screen, so it may be necessary
to move the OHP further back in order to produce a screen size large
enough for all students to clearly see the projection. Depending on the
room layout, it may not always be possible to produce an ideal projection in the centre of the room, so it may be a case of compromise.

However, you should not be discouraged from moving furniture around or possibly using the OHP to one side of the room if it helps increase visibility.

Another aspect of screen focus that sometimes occurs is the phenomenon of chromatic aberration, characterised by coloured areas towards the edge of the projected image that encroaches on available viewing area. Many modern OHPs have an adjuster that can reduce or clear this effect.

Producing a clear display image

If an OHP is not projected squarely onto a screen, you can get a distorted image, referred to as 'keystoning'. Figure 3.3 shows this effect. Keystoning will arise if the OHP shines onto the display screen at an angle. To avoid this problem, make sure that the OHP is directly in front of the screen and, if the problem persists, you may need to adjust the screen itself to a slight angle.

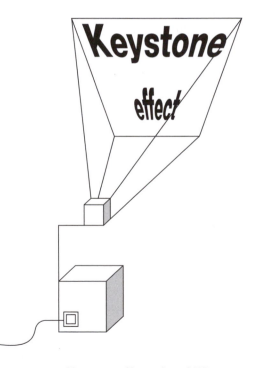

FIGURE 3.3 Keystone effect of an OHP

If the OHP is situated directly in front of the display screen and there is still a keystoning effect, it is usually because the projector display lens (the head of the projector) is too low. Although raising the OHP will minimise this problem, it can also lead to the 'arm' of the projector (supporting the lens) blocking the students' view. Therefore, if you have an adjustable screen, you should try to tilt the screen forward to reduce the keystoning effect.

One final consideration when ensuring a clear image from an OHP is to make sure that the OHP and its lens are clean and clear of marks or dust. What may appear as a small speck on the OHP can be magnified in the final display and can distract the students more than you realise. It is fairly straightforward to clean the OHP surfaces with a dry cloth or tissue, but you should take care not to smear grease on the OHP. To clean such smears it may be worth occasionally using a spirit-based cleaner.

Document projectors and display area

You may find yourself teaching in a lecture theatre which has been specially fitted with a wide range of technology to aid lectures. One

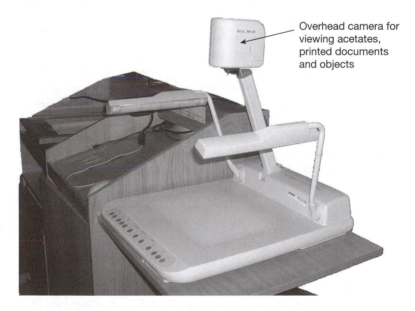

Overhead camera for viewing acetates, printed documents and objects

FIGURE 3.4 Document projector

such piece of equipment might be a document projector (Figure 3.4). This equipment allows paper (i.e. printed) documents and other, three-dimensional, objects to be displayed using an overhead light source to illuminate the text or object for a camera. The camera is then linked to the projection facility to display the printed document or object. This equipment also doubles up as an OHP using a light source below to show the acetate.

Although this is a handy tool for displaying printed documents and objects, the make-up of the equipment often means that the display area is less than A4 size. This can prove awkward if you are trying to show an acetate which has been set up for full viewing at A4, i.e. portrait layout, especially if you are trying to show a diagram. Another issue with this equipment is that, because it has a dual function, the quality of the displayed image can be poorer than a dedicated OHP.

PRODUCING OVERHEAD TRANSPARENCIES (ACETATES)

Handwritten notes versus printed notes

Acetates come in two basic forms: as a long continuous roll of acetate and as single A4 sheets. Rolls of acetate can obviously store a lot more information than a single sheet and some lecturers used to (and may still do) prepare their notes on rolls and bring them to the classroom with them. This produces several problems: the first is that invariably the notes have to be handwritten and hence there is a reliance on the lecturer having neat, clear handwriting; secondly, since the acetate is rolled up, the content will rub and will eventually be smudged; finally, many OHPs do not have roll holders to support the acetate roll. Therefore this is not a recommended approach.

It would generally be advisable to avoid handwriting on acetate sheets. Unless the lecturer has very clear and tidy handwriting, the students may have difficulty reading it. Also, handwritten acetates can appear unprofessional, suggesting a lack of preparation.

Word processing your notes

These days most people should have at least some IT skills that enable them to undertake basic word processing. Therefore, it is not too diffi-cult to type up a set of basic key points relating to your lecture notes which can then be printed and photocopied onto acetates. The result is that you have legible and professional-looking visual aids for use in your teaching. It is also possible to print directly onto acetate sheets, but this requires special quality acetate that has a rough surface capable of adsorbing the ink. Colour acetates can be printed using an inkjet printer, but be careful about the overuse of colour as colour ink can prove expensive.

A special note should be made here about photocopying onto acetate. Photocopiers use a toner powder which is imprinted onto the material under high temperatures. Therefore, only special acetate sheets which are capable of withstanding high temperatures should be used for photocopying. Otherwise the acetate may melt and damage the photocopier.

Another advantage of printing out your notes and photocopying them onto acetate is the fact that you have a paper version of your notes in the correct order that can be used for reference. This can be useful after a lecture when you reorganise and order your acetates ready for filing.

USING ACETATES

Making the content visible

There are two common methods for showing an acetate: (i) all at once; or (ii) a part at a time. If you show an acetate bit by bit, by the process of revelation, you can use a number of methods. The simplest and most common method is to use a piece of paper to uncover the acetate as you go along. A potential problem with this method is that the paper can keep slipping, especially if the OHP cooling fan keeps blowing the paper away. This means that your attempts to keep content hidden becomes a distraction from the actual point being made. If you favour this approach, then you should take care to secure the paper with, say, a pen or other sturdy object that will hold the cover in place until you are ready to reveal the additional content. Alternatively, a quick tip is to place the paper under the acetate to help hold it in place.

In some circumstances this may not be appropriate, especially if you have a diagram or chart. Therefore, you can reveal content by selectively removing covers which may be attached to the edge of the acetate, or even use post-it notes which can be revealed in sequence. Conversely, you may choose to build up the acetate by placing successive sheets or overlays on top of each other. One difficulty with this approach, however, is that the overall image may become distorted through the several layers of acetate and, if two objects need to be placed very closely together, it may be too difficult to line things up accurately. An alternative would be to replace the acetate each time with another that progressively shows the extra information.

While these methods can be useful, they can also prove counter-productive to the learning process if used excessively. Students may feel that they are being controlled too much in what they are and aren't allowed to see. Also, while gradual exposure of the content can help focus the student on the point in question, some students can also be distracted by thinking about what will come next, almost by trying to second-guess the content.

Sometimes it is actually better to show the entire content at once so that the students see the whole format of the content, otherwise it may be difficult for students to grasp an understanding of the wider issues being discussed. Therefore, a good medium can be struck by employing different approaches according to the circumstances.

Writing on acetates

The merits of handwriting your notes as opposed to printing them were discussed earlier, with the recommendation that you should avoid handwritten notes. However, there are times when handwriting in front of the students in real time can be helpful, for example when working through a calculation as you explain the process step by step. Do remember to use a permanent marker so that your notes are much less susceptible to smudging. In addition, you may wish to use a non-permanent marker during class so that if you need to jot down a few temporary notes, they can be easily removed afterwards, leaving your original notes intact. It is easier for your students to read your notes if you use black or dark blue for the main text, only using red and green to highlight points.

Displaying an acetate

Even if an acetate has been prepared with care, it is of little use if the students cannot see it. The first thing you should do at the start of class is to test the OHP and check that the content is visible from the back of the room. When showing acetates, you should also be conscious of where you stand so that you do not block the students' view of the display screen. If necessary, stand well away from the projection area for a moment to allow students time to view the content.

If you need to point at something being displayed, try to point at the object on the display area rather than at the actual acetate. If you try to point at the acetate itself, it means you have to be standing beside the OHP, and that means you are more likely to block someone's view. Alternatively, place an object such as a pen on the acetate that points at the object or image being discussed. When you have finished showing your acetates, or even if you switch focus from the acetate for several minutes, you should always turn the OHP off. This avoids students being distracted by continuing to look at the acetate when you actually want them to focus on something else, and also reduces the noise produced by the OHP.

Pointing straight at the display might seem difficult if the projection area is quite large but there are a couple of ways of circumventing this. Laser pointers, which are now cheaply available, can produce a red beam of light that can be pointed at the screen. These are so common they can even be bought as laser key rings. An alternative is the traditional 'teacher's stick', often a bamboo cane, although it would be impractical to carry one of these to every lecture. However, it is also possible to purchase telescopic pointers that resemble car or radio aerials. When collapsed, they look like a pen and are very compact and portable.

Presenting an acetate

How often do you quickly display an acetate and then pull it away again? If so, what is the purpose of showing it? The function of an acetate should be explained to the students so they know what to expect. For example, are they expected to copy what is presented and, if so, they should therefore be given plenty of time to take notes. Another mistake people often make is to continue talking while the students are taking notes. Most, if not all, students are incapable of taking comprehensive notes and listening to the teacher at the same time. They will either be able to listen to what you are saying or be able to take notes but not both, so you should explain what you expect from the students. If you want them to take notes, say so and don't speak while they're writing, or explain that they shouldn't write but listen instead.

POWERPOINT PRESENTATIONS

What is PowerPoint?

PowerPoint is produced by Microsoft and is an example of a computer-based presentation software package. Although there are a number of other presentation packages available on the market, PowerPoint has become the de facto industry standard that most people are familiar with. At its most basic level, a PowerPoint presentation can be delivered much the same way as you would deliver overhead transparencies, but with the benefit of automated transition between each slide.

The ethos of a PowerPoint presentation is built around that of a 35 mm slide show. By default each PowerPoint 'slide' is the same shape as a 35 mm slide projection and slide transition from one to the next can be controlled by a click of the mouse on the computer. The added advantage is that you have a range of interactive features, whereas a traditional slide is a static image.

Advantages of using PowerPoint

Apart from improving the quality of your presentation and the delivery of content, using PowerPoint also has a number of additional advantages. If you re-use content for different classes and/or students, then, as with many people, you don't always cover exactly the same content each time. This means that students being exposed to the same content may experience different learning experiences. By using the same presentation as an aid to your teaching, you are more likely to ensure a consistent delivery, providing equality of the learning experience and making sure you never forget to mention pertinent points.

With the increase in electronic support for students, especially via the Internet, it is now possible to make resources more easily accessible for students. Since PowerPoint is a computer-based technology, it is possible to make copies of your presentation available to students as a revision aid, or to allow students to access lecture notes which they may have missed in class through illness or some other valid reason.

Providing access to such resources also holds the potential to increase the learning process for students. Some students may have difficulty concentrating in class or will not have time to digest the content being shown. By gaining access to resources over the Internet, say, they can then review the material as many times as they like and revisit topics they did not understand. Due to the interactive nature of PowerPoint, it is also possible to adapt notes to question the students and get them thinking about key topics.

A cautionary note about PowerPoint

Although PowerPoint has many advantages, a note of caution should also be raised, since PowerPoint can be used inappropriately to produce bad presentations. One of the strengths of PowerPoint is its ease of use and the ability to add text animations and sound effects. However, as mentioned with the use of acetates, the important aspect is the content. Therefore, it can sometimes be tempting to add extra animations and sounds which make the presentation seem more appealing, but at times this only distracts the students' attention from the content. Therefore, many features in PowerPoint should be avoided for academic purposes or used only when they enhance the content.

Many people only ever use the basic features of PowerPoint but, even at this level, it is still easy to create a poor presentation. The more choices you are given, the more complex and potentially problematic things can be. While PowerPoint offers a wide range of background designs and animation features, many of the options available are simply not suitable for formal lectures. Also, inappropriate use of audio such as a bullet ricochet sound for each new key point, only distracts the student from the content. The intention is not to leave the students wondering 'How do you do that?' but to be focused on the content. Therefore, the fundamental message when using PowerPoint is to *keep it simple*.

What can you do with PowerPoint?

Slide shows

The most basic use of PowerPoint would be to show slides that can be shown in succession. Building on this, it is possible to make the content more visually appealing by adding coloured backgrounds and interesting designs, all of which come with the software as standard. Using the same method of revelation as with acetates, where content is revealed bit by bit, it is possible to build up each key point one by one using built-in animations, as well as changing from slide to slide using slide transition graphics. Although these animations can also be accompanied by sound effects to make the presentation more 'interesting', sound effects should actually be avoided or only used sparingly to emphasise particular points.

Adding graphics

It is easy to add graphics to a PowerPoint presentation and there are several options for doing this. It is possible to produce simple diagrams using the drawing tools available within PowerPoint, although it is just as easy to 'copy and paste' a diagram or image created using other software. Digital scanners (equipment that can digitise images and store them on computer) are now widely available and can be used to scan images, photos and other objects, which can then be incorporated into a presentation.

Although it is just as easy to show images, diagrams etc. on an acetate, the added advantage here is that the presentation of the content can be more interactive. Images can be revealed at appropriate moments and modified in stages to help students understand the topic. PowerPoint also enables these diagrams to be turned into simple animations, along the lines of the old style 'flick books' where a series of static images are displayed in quick succession to give the impression of movement. This can be useful, for example, when demonstrating how a moving part works in an internal combustion engine, or the flow of information in a business model.

Multimedia presentations

Since PowerPoint is a software package, it has facilities to incorporate a number of other media forms that can be utilised by a computer. Audio can easily be incorporated into a slide show and this can add to the learning experience for the students. Examples include:

- bird songs to compare signal intentions in mating calls or warning signals;
- brief conversations to demonstrate particular points to language students; or
- pulse sounds or breathing differences in patients for medical students.

 30

Possibly the most complex option in PowerPoint is the inclusion of video. In a similar way to audio clips, it is possible to include video clips as part of a presentation. As with video viewed through a television, the possibilities are endless in terms of teaching and learning opportunities but the same principles should be applied as if displaying a simple text bullet point. The video clip should be an aid to the overall content and should serve a purpose. To hold attention, it is best to keep video clips short within a presentation and to ask the students to look for particular points given in question sheets. The use of video and question sheets is covered in more detail in Chapter 5.

By using a combination of some or all of the options available in PowerPoint, it is possible to develop fully interactive multimedia presentations. These presentations can help the students understand concepts which might otherwise be difficult to grasp if explained by word of mouth. The important caveat, however, is that the content should always be the central focus and not the technology itself.

CREATING A POWERPOINT PRESENTATION

One reason for using modern technology is to make a task quicker or more straightforward. PowerPoint does this by adopting various standards necessary for a good presentation, such as having bullet points as standard and using a default font size that will be easily visible. It also offers a range of presentation styles and animation options that can be quickly selected. Therefore, to create a basic presentation you need do little more than type in your text. It even tells you where to click to add the text.

As with any teaching notes, the content for a presentation should be thought out carefully with a clear structure to the format. This should cover an overall view of the content and have individual topics referenced. Many teachers now often prepare their lecture notes in word processing packages and so already have electronic notes to hand. It is therefore quite straightforward to simply copy and paste key points into PowerPoint that reflect the existing format of their lecture notes. With more experience it will then become easier to prepare lecture notes directly in PowerPoint rather than copy them from a word processor.

Creating handouts and slides from PowerPoint

PowerPoint offers several printing options when working with presentations. An existing presentation can simply be printed, but there is also an option to produce a set of notes to accompany the slide printouts. This enables you to use the printouts as an aide memoire for your presentation, showing each slide with its accompanying lecture notes. If the presentation contains straightforward content, it is possible to print a set of slides that provides space for students to make supplementary notes (see Figure 3.5) so that more time can be spent discussing the content during class. The slides can then be added to by the students and built up into a detailed set of lecture support notes.

Why should I use IT?

Pros	Cons
Saves time	Takes up time
Enhances learning	Doesn't enhance learning
Accommodates more students	Student access is limited
It's cheaper	It's expensive
It's innovative	It's mundane
It's easy to use	It requires technical expertise

The possibilities

- Presentations
- Instructional programs
- Revision aids/analysis programs
- Simulations
- CMC
- Virtual environments
- WWW

How do I find resources?

- LTSN centres
- Online magazines (deliberations)
- Email lists (jiscmail)
- Online resources (BUBL)
- Commercial publishers (Taylor & Francis)
- Word of mouth

■ **FIGURE 3.5** Image of PowerPoint handout allowing space for student notes

■ 32

Since PowerPoint presentations are designed along the same lines as a traditional slide show, it would make sense if you could also produce proper 35 mm slides from a presentation. PowerPoint presentations can therefore be transformed into ordinary 35 mm slides using something called a film recorder, which is discussed in further detail in Chapter 5.

A film recorder is connected to a computer and dedicated software helps turn each PowerPoint slide into a photographic image on film. Since the presentation already exists in digital format on a computer, the film recorder can 'photograph' each slide onto the 35 mm film and turn it into a slide. Having a set of slides of your presentation may be useful if you want to give a talk where only a traditional slide projector is available.

Using the computer, it is possible to produce and edit digital images and diagrams before they are turned into slides. This allows you to emphasise parts of an image, for example, by adding labels.

Things to consider

PowerPoint incorporates some basic presentation guidelines automatically without the user necessarily being aware of them. Such things cover font size and visual appeal, but if you refer back to the points described for overhead transparencies (acetates), you will find that they have a lot in common (see Figure 3.1). This is because the end result is the same, content being displayed onto a display area which has to be visible and interesting for the students to read. Therefore, there are certain dos and don'ts that you should be aware of when working with PowerPoint.

Do

- consider purpose, e.g. aid to note taking;
- consider font, colour, legibility etc.;
- be consistent with layout.

Don't

- keep changing styles/backgrounds;
- get carried away with animations;
- rely on the projected image display looking exactly the same as the computer monitor.

33

Avoid using pale colours for a PowerPoint presentation as they are likely to appear slightly faded or 'washed out' in comparison to the computer display.

SUMMARY

Using an overhead projector

- Prepare your acetates in advance;
- check that the equipment works;
- preview the first acetate on the OHP prior to class and check that it is visible from the back of the room;
- don't obstruct the students' view;
- explain the function of the acetate;
- give students time to write notes and don't talk at the same time;
- use the OHP to engage your students and don't just use it as an alternative to you talking.

Using PowerPoint

- Prepare your presentation in advance;
- check that the equipment works;
- make sure the presentation is visible from the back of the room;
- have a contingency plan in case the equipment doesn't work - prepare some acetates or handouts.

Data projectors

A data projector is a display tool for projecting the display from a computer screen or a video programme onto a large viewing surface for audiences. The computer or video player is simply plugged into the data projector and the output (computer screen or video) is projected onto a large screen for easy viewing by the audience. Data projectors are relatively cheap and many institutions have them permanently available in lecture theatres or teaching rooms as standard audio-visual display equipment.

Although not essential for displaying video, data projectors are essential if you wish to display a PowerPoint presentation as it would be

FIGURE 3.6 Portable data projector

impractical to run a presentation and expect students to view it directly from the computer screen. The advantage of using a data projector for viewing videos, however, is that you do not need to use a television and the projected video image can be much larger than the image produced by a television, even a large screen television.

Data projectors and video players are available as portable units (Figure 3.6) and so it is now quite easy to give PowerPoint presentations or play a video wherever you go. If the room you are teaching in has no data projector available, it is quite straightforward to bring one along and plug it into a video player or computer for use with your students.

USING AN OHP AND POWERPOINT IN THE DISCIPLINES

While not a subject specific example, Figure 3.7 shows two overhead transparencies that demonstrate how to present key points. Although not to scale, they show that large fonts have been used, key points as opposed to full sentences have been used, and that the number of bullet points have been kept to a minimum. The actual points themselves provide a checklist for good practice when using acetates.

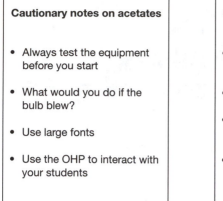

FIGURE 3.7 Sample acetates showing how to highlight key points

Topics for discussion

- Analyse the sales trends in this graph
- What was the reason for the dip in 1996?
- What does the overall trend indicate and what are the reasons for this?

FIGURE 3.8 PowerPoint slide used to prompt student responses

The slide shown in Figure 3.8 is a very simple example of how PowerPoint can be used to encourage responses from the students in class. This way, the presentation changes from a passive medium into an interactive one where students have to respond to questions and information provided by the teacher. Again, this slide is not to scale so the text and graph will appear more legible when displayed through a projector.

FURTHER READING

Brown, George and Atkins, Madeleine (1988) *Effective Teaching in Higher Education* (first published, London: Methuen; reprinted 1997, London: Routledge).

O'Hagan, Chris (1998) *Staff Development for Teaching and Learning Technology: Ten Keys to Success*, UCoSDA Briefing Paper 53, January (UCoSDA is now known as Higher Education Staff Development Agency, HESDA, http://www. hesda.org.uk/index.html).

Chapter 4

Handouts

Handouts have long been a mainstay for providing students with information to support face-to-face teaching. Early efforts often consisted of handwritten notes that were photocopied, or clippings of text and images that were glued together and then photocopied. However, after several times through the copier, these notes and images often ended up as vague dark blobs that were difficult to decipher. With computer technology advancing so much in recent years, it is now possible to produce legible and professional-looking handouts quite easily. But the other important consideration when producing good handouts is preparation.

The students were always provided with a comprehensive set of handouts

When preparing handouts for students it is important to consider your reasons for producing them in the first place. There are a number of benefits to planning your handouts. It is more professional to produce clear handouts and this serves as a good example to students for presenting their own work. A handout with a clear purpose will mean fewer requests from students for clarification and, if the material is of clear benefit to the students, they are more likely to use it.

The last statement may seem obvious, but it is an unfortunate truth that many handouts end up among student notes without ever being read or used to support their studies. The aim of this chapter is to give some guidelines on how to plan effective handouts which are well prepared and well presented through the support of C&IT so that students are more likely to make effective use of them.

WHAT MAKES A GOOD HANDOUT?

A good handout should:

- serve a purpose for both the students *and* the teacher;
- enhance rather than replace teaching;
- aid or replace unnecessary note taking;
- act as a starting point for further study and research;
- provide information without spoon feeding;
- be capable of being easily assimilated by students at the beginning of the teaching session.

When thinking about a purpose for your handouts, there are a number of issues you need to consider:

- will they mainly act as a source of information?
- will they support note taking during class?
- are they intended to replace note taking?
- are students likely to miss the lecture if comprehensive handouts are available?
- how will the handouts be introduced, at the start or end of class?
- will the handouts be incorporated into class activities?
- will they provide background content so that lecture time can be used more creatively?

THE BENEFITS OF USING HANDOUTS

Maintaining student interest

Student attention often only lasts about fifteen to twenty minutes at best before interest wanes and the ability to learn and recall information diminishes. The strategic use of handouts during a lecture can help maintain student interest by switching their attention from one activity to another. This helps account for the fifteen-to-twenty-minute concentration cycle so that the students will have the potential to retain more of the information based on known learning patterns. Even the process of distributing a handout in class, which will take a minute or two, is sometimes long enough for students to re-focus their attention back onto you when you start talking again.

Aid to note taking

Perhaps one of the most common problems that students face during a lecture is trying to take comprehensive notes and listen to the teacher at the same time. An old joke suggests that the definition of a lecture is 'the transfer of information from the lecturer's notes to the students' notes without passing through the brains of either'. By providing handouts the teacher can ensure that students are able to listen attentively and learn instead of just trying to write everything down.

If part of a lecture is straightforward information delivery, then there is little point in wasting time getting students to copy the information down. There is also the potential problem that students won't reproduce identical notes, missing important points or misinterpreting explanations. By providing this information in handout form, the time saved during class can be used for other activities such as exercises or group discussions.

Class activities

The use of handouts in a lecture can be used as a basis of a variety of activities that result in an interactive session. For example, handouts can provide 'prompter' questions that can be used to initiate student discussion. Alternatively, students can be given simple exercises to work through either individually or in groups and then model answers or key issues can be drawn out by the teacher in front of the whole class. This process enables the students to explore problems and obtain instant feedback during class.

Another use is to provide students with incomplete sets of lecture notes which have to be completed by the students during the lecture. You can then spend more time discussing a topic and the few notes students do have to make will be more informed by discussion. An advantage of this is that since the notes are incomplete, students still have the incentive to attend the lecture in order to gain a full set of notes.

Worksheets

Handouts can be given in the form of worksheets that act as precursors to additional work, some of which may be continued after class. Students can be set tasks or problems and the lecture may be used to provide initial information which leads to further study or research. For example, a topic may be introduced during the lecture with a few key examples and references. A worksheet could be provided with additional information and questions which the students would then have to research before the next class. This work could then be used as the starting point for the next lecture, initiated by student feedback on the activities and to provide help for any problems the students may have had.

USING TECHNOLOGY TO PRODUCE HANDOUTS

Since handouts are paper-based, it may seem strange to consider the role of C&IT, but there are a number of benefits. The most obvious one is that there is an electronic record of the content, so if the original handouts are lost or damaged, you can always quickly print another set. The second major advantage is that C&IT can be used to prepare and design professional-looking handouts. The third advantage is the ability to easily update the content and provide quick access for students through various electronic distribution routes.

Probably the most fundamental advantage of using technology to produce handouts is that the text is typed up rather than handwritten and so will be legible when printed. Handwritten notes should never be distributed as a handout because of the problems of legibility and updating, and also because they do not appear professional. Students may view the hurried impression created by using handwritten notes with disdain.

There are several software packages on the market that allow you to produce professional-looking handout documents, similar to professional desktop publishing. This allows the author to organise text into different formats, such as in columns, or to insert images and wrap text around them, in the same way you see articles in newspapers or magazines. It is also straightforward to add annotations, draw diagrams and label images that can then be placed anywhere on the page. While this may appear very complicated, requiring extensive computer skills, most word processors also offer this functionality. Therefore, with only basic word processing skills and, perhaps, a little practice, most people can produce this sort of work.

A cautionary note about handouts

While handouts can have a range of uses, if not thought out properly their usefulness is quickly lost. If the purpose of the handout is not explained and the content is not closely tied in with the lecture materials, students simply won't read them. Also, if the handout is poorly designed and presented, perhaps with too much text or no explanation of how to use the material, students will not easily digest the content.

Another problem with the use of handouts is information overload. If students are simply given too many handouts, they will not be able to digest all the material. Also, there is the potential issue of copyright infringement. Within the current regulations of fair use, it is acceptable for a teacher to photocopy journal and periodical articles or sections of a textbook, although copyright clearance should be checked on exactly what is allowed for teaching purposes.

However, specific copyright clearance must be sought for resource packs, which are classed as twenty-five pages or more of copied material. Many teachers may think this issue does not apply to them, but if you progressively photocopy materials for your students throughout a module or course and these add up to more than twenty-five pages, they constitute a resource pack for that module or course, regardless of whether or not the content was issued in one go. Therefore, it is important to be aware of where materials are collected from for inclusion in handouts.

Many teachers may have inadvertently infringed copyright in a lecture when supplying handouts, but with the advent of the Web and the ease by which these resources can be made universally available online, there is a greater risk of perpetuating copyright infringements. Therefore, you should be careful about what content you include in your handouts. However, there are also increasing volumes of good quality resources now freely available for use in education and Chapter 7, on electronic information resources, provides advice on locating these.

PREPARING HANDOUTS

Although handouts are possibly the easiest type of resource to produce – you can simply photocopy text and distribute it – a handout needs to be planned carefully if it is to be a useful resource. There are four aspects to producing handouts:

1 purpose;
2 content;
3 design;
4 presentation.

Purpose

The aims and objectives, or learning outcomes, should be identified before any materials are produced. By knowing what you want the students to gain from using the handouts, you will know what you need to put in. Once the purpose has been established, it is then easier to develop the content.

The purpose for the handouts should be quite clear to you and, therefore, to the students. Students should know what the handouts are for, how they should be used and how they fit with the lectures or classes where they were handed out. One particular advantage of a handout is to act as an aid to note taking. Rather than spend time writing copious amounts of notes, students can spend more time listening to the teacher about the subject.

As part of the preparation for producing handouts, it is also important to be aware of the profile of your students, so that you can tailor the material more appropriately to their needs. Try to build a better understanding of the student profile: consider, for example, their background knowledge, individual circumstances (mature students, level one or final year), motivation (is it an applied course or more theoretical?), and preferred learning styles.

Content

Having identified a clear purpose for producing a handout, the content can be planned with a clear goal. When considering the content, you need to decide what the main themes and topics will cover. Knowing the student profile will help you pitch the material at the right level. The content should therefore be useful and relevant for the student. For example, what skills or knowledge are the students likely to have and will the handout take this into account? Generally, it is probably better to provide some information which might be familiar to the students rather than risk leaving holes or gaps which may not be covered appropriately elsewhere.

The structure of the content is a key factor in how well the students are able to digest the material. If the structure is systematic, students can develop a clear picture of how different topics fit together. Since much of the handout is going to be read away from the class, the students should still be able to follow the message being conveyed. It should be clear how the content is subdivided and where the key points are given. One way to help students link handouts together into a structure they can follow is to colour code sections, or add dates so they know how the content fits together.

Design

The appearance of a handout is important, so it must be designed for both visual appeal and maximum readability. When students pick up a handout it should not put them off reading it, but should be laid out in an open and inviting format. If you are providing textual information it should be easy to read, so do not put too much text onto one page or provide endless reams of text. A handout should not be a mini textbook.

The use of images can help visualise concepts and is more appealing than just text descriptions. Images also help break up sections of text, which can also help the design. It is helpful to have some 'white space' on a page, i.e. blank space with no content. Again, this breaks up the structure of the handout to make it easier to read, but it also provides space for students to add notes and comments.

When designing a handout, it is also helpful to be creative and not simply reproduce a book format. Images help visual appeal, but you can also consider making key headings stand out more, rather like reference points to the detailed text, or perhaps split the text into columns at times. However, certain design features are subjective, so be careful not to get so carried away that the main point of the handout, i.e. the content, is not lost to an excessive use of gimmicks.

Presentation

If a handout is well designed, it mostly follows that the presentation will also be well presented. A well-presented handout will have a proper structure so that the student understands the purpose of the handout from the format of the headings, text etc. Text should be presented in a good size font, no smaller than 12 point, and images should be clearly labelled and referenced appropriately in the text. Other information such as references should also be properly presented, making no assumptions that students will know the abbreviations of journals etc.

Another small but relevant point about presentation is the justification of text. Many people fully justify text so that it is flush with the left and right sides of the page or margin. While this often makes the text look more presentable, it can actually put some students off. Some dyslexic students, as well as other readers, are put off by justified text because it provides no visual markers from reading line to line. Left-justified text leaves 'jagged' lines, but these provide good markers for reading text. Therefore, while it may appear more presentable, text is more readable if it is not fully justified.

PRODUCING HANDOUTS

Figure 4.1 summarises the basic steps for producing handouts. The planning and preparation should be factored into the work and not be an afterthought. This will ensure that the students are able to gain real benefits from any materials produced. When writing the content it should be informal and in the first person, as if you are talking to the student. This makes the content more appealing to the student and more readable.

Each person has their own writing style, so once you have written your notes it is important to get them proof-read independently. By doing this you are able to seek independent advice to clarify whether what you have written actually comes across to the reader just as clearly. This is an iterative process and may take several attempts before the content is deemed acceptable for use by students.

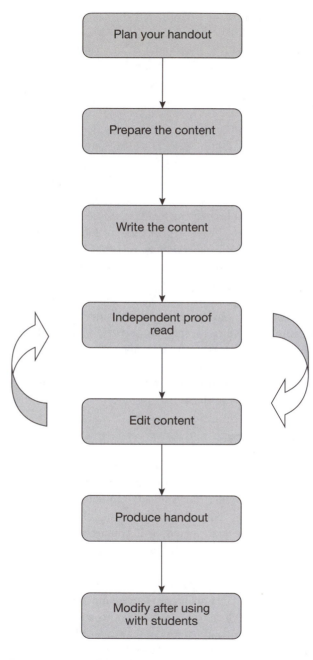

FIGURE 4.1 Flowchart for producing handouts

Although the content may actually be quite technical or require a good understanding of the subject, it is often very useful to ask an independent (non-specialist) colleague or friend to proof read the material. They will not only help pick up typographical errors, but they are also likely to ask basic questions such as 'Will the students know that term?' or 'What is meant by?'. This can often be very enlightening as many of us easily make assumptions that the students will understand terms and concepts that we take for granted.

In addition, an independent proof read provides checks on your writing style just in case you may appear slightly patronising or too informal. Other aspects of your writing style to check include:

- Are my notes too verbose?
- Are my sentences too long or too short?
- Do I use colloquialisms?
- Do I keep repeating common terms or phrases?
- Do I assume that students will understand technical terms?

Taking these points into consideration may seem extreme at times but with the globalisation of education, many courses now regularly enlist students whose first language is not English. Therefore, by taking time to check your content, you avoid any potential misunderstandings that can confuse students.

Producing worksheets

Worksheets are a form of handout which promote activities and exercises that help students explore a subject or topic in greater depth and understanding. The first consideration when designing and producing a worksheet as a handout is to decide on the purpose for its use. Since the students will be expected to engage in structured exercises, you should therefore provide clear instructions. Terms such as 'explore', 'consider' or 'discuss' should be avoided unless they are put into context of the overall exercise outlined in the worksheet. Explicit learning outcomes should therefore be outlined so that students are clear about what it is they should be working towards.

Worksheets can cover a range of activities such as 'prompter' questions to get students thinking about key issues, or as the basis of discussion to tease out various aspects of a topic. A common form of worksheet can be produced as a question sheet, where students are simply given questions which they have to answer. This can include straightforward answers to numerical or factual questions, or more subjective questions requiring open-ended discursive responses.

It is possible to design worksheets to act as a precursor for further study and research on a topic. The worksheet can be designed to provide rudimentary information about a topic, giving some fundamental terms and references. Further study can be encouraged by asking questions such as 'What is the definition of?' or 'What other key issues relate to?'. In addition, activities such as 'Name two further examples of' or 'List other instances of' can be used to encourage further research on a topic. Examples of worksheets to support teaching and learning are provided in the next chapter on using video in the classroom.

USING HANDOUTS IN THE DISCIPLINES

The following examples demonstrate different uses for handouts in several subject areas. Two of the examples have been adapted from ones cited in support notes produced by the Educational Development Team, University of Hull.

Introduction to microbiology

This handout (see p. 49) has a primary purpose as an aid to note taking:

- The instructions say what is covered in a logical order;
- there are gaps in the notes so students can complete sections;
- the students do not need to write full notes for the lectures;
- further reading is prompted with specific questions.

The design of this handout means that any students who miss the class will still be able to benefit from the material although they will need to do some further work, so the incentive to attend the lecture is still there.

Italian Renaissance art

This handout (see p. 50) is aimed at information delivery and is clearly structured. It informs the students what will be covered during the lecture and how the content will fit in with the rest of the lecture course. By providing examples of the works discussed, it provides correct references, acknowledging that students don't always write accurate notes.

Introduction to microbiology

This lecture is designed to introduce you to basic microbiology, covering standard terminology, fundamental morphology and basic types of microscope.

By the end of the lecture you should:

- Understand key terms used in microbiology
- Understand what morphology is and be able to describe basic types of microorganism
- Be able to list the different types of microscope used for viewing microorganisms
- Have a basic understanding of how different types of microscope work

Reading list
Microbiology an Introduction 7th edn, Gerard J Tortora, Berdell R Funke, Christine L Case (2001), Benjamin Cummings
Biology of Microorganisms 9th edn, Brock (2000), Prentice Hall

Morphology is . . .

There are three basic forms of bacteria:

1. **coccus.** These cells are fairly circular in shape and may form long chains or clusters:

2. **bacillus.** These cells tend to be rod shaped.

3. List the other main type of bacterium and draw its shape:

Microscopes
There are several types of microscope:

- Compound (optical) microscope
- Phase contrast microscope

What other basic type of microscope is there?

Produce notes of no more than 300 words on how a phase contrast microscope works

Italian Renaissance art

Lecture 2 Sculpture – Ghiberti and Donatello

Subject
An introduction to early Florentine Renaissance sculpture based on works by two leading artists. One, Ghiberti, in many ways a transitional figure. The other, Donatello, one of the most revolutionary and influential artists of the Renaissance.

Aims
The lecture is intended to build on the previous lecture introducing the Florentine Renaissance, by providing a general view of developments in sculpture in the early Renaissance. It also seeks to introduce some of the themes and topics we will be developing later in the course and more specifically to prepare the ground for the seminars on the Cantorie (singing galleries).

Objectives
By the end of the lecture you should have:

- Gained a broad outline of the development of early Renaissance sculpture in Florence
- Been introduced to the artistic style of Ghiberti and Donatello
- Gained a better understanding of the form, function and context of their works
- Been introduced to topics to be developed in later lectures and seminars

The particular works discussed include:

Andrea Pisano (recorded 1330–48?)
Baptistery Doors (bronze), 1330–36, south doors Baptistery, Florence

Brunelleschi (1317–1446)
Sacrifice of Isaac (bronze competition relief), 1401 (Bargello Museum, Florence)

Lorenzo Ghiberti
Sacrifice of Isaac (bronze competition relief), 1401 (Bargello Museum, Florence)

Baptistery Doors (bronze), 1403–24, north doors Baptistery, Florence

St John Baptist (bronze), 1412–14, Or San Michele, for Arte del Calimala

St Matthew (bronze), 1419–22, Or San Michele, for Arte del Cambrio (bankers)

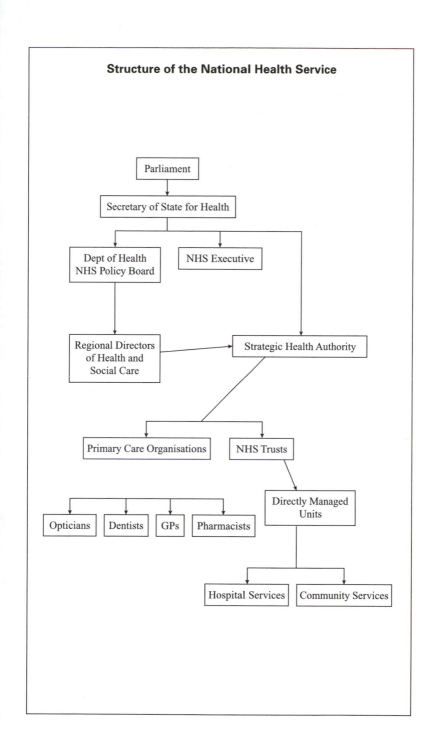

Structure of the National Health Service

Parliament

Secretary of State for Health

Dept of Health
NHS Policy Board

NHS Executive

Regional Directors
of Health and
Social Care

Strategic Health Authority

Primary Care Organisations

NHS Trusts

Opticians

Dentists

GPs

Pharmacists

Directly Managed
Units

Hospital Services

Community Services

Structure of the National Health Service

The National Health Service is a complex system and it is difficult for students to understand the structure without the aid of a diagram. The handout shown on p. 51 is a basic representation of the NHS to help students visualise the structure.

📖 FURTHER READING

Computer Assisted Assessment Centre, available online at http://www. caacentre.ac.uk (accessed 04/08/03).

Habeshaw, Trevor, Habeshaw, Sue and Gibbs, Graham (1995) *53 Interesting Ways of Helping Your Students to Study*, Bristol: Technical and Educational Services.

Chapter 5

Videos and slides[1]

IS VIDEO THE LAST BASTION OF THE POOR TEACHER?

The use of video and television programmes in the classroom became relatively commonplace way back in the 1960s and 1970s. As with any new technology of the time, many people quickly adopted its use for a whole range of purposes. It even became a mainstay of content delivery for the Open University on late night or early morning showing via the BBC. Such was the impact of this mode of delivery that the archetypal image of the Open University presenter became that of a bearded professor with a kipper tie and tweed jacket with leather elbow patches, so often parodied in British comedy and culture.

The downside of this, however, was that the use of video was often employed as a teaching and learning tool by teachers who didn't know how to use it to its full potential. In addition, many used video in the classroom as a passive teaching medium, expecting the students somehow to 'absorb' the content simply because they were sitting in front of the television.

Video was also used for inappropriate purposes such as rewards for students who were often promised a video 'if they were good'. In conjunction with this, video became a measure of discipline to pacify students as a way of 'keeping them quiet'. This also meant extra breathing space for the teacher, who didn't have to engage the students while the video was playing, or have to provide any follow-up activities.

---

[1] For the context of this chapter the term 'video' is used to refer to any form of televisual programme delivered through the medium of television, irrespective of whether it is a video film, pre-recorded programme or even live broadcast.

Professor Tweed started the television programme with a relatively simple equation

Consequently, the rationale grew that a teacher could hide behind the use of video, not as an aid to teaching and learning, but as a means of controlling students and deflecting attention from any possibly weak teaching abilities. The result was that the use of video in the classroom became somewhat unpopular due to the stigma attached to it.

While this was certainly true in some cases, and many people may be able to recall similar incidents from their own educational experiences, it is an unfair reflection on the real potential of video as an interactive teaching and learning tool. Coming full circle, video can therefore actually be a very useful teaching aid, provided its use is well thought out, rather than something to hide behind.

ADVANTAGES OF USING VIDEO

There is a wide range of reasons for using video. Depending on the teaching approach adopted, there is also a wide range of benefits to be gained.

Motivation

Even the best teacher in the world can find it difficult to motivate students if the same teaching method is employed week in, week out. By using video it is possible to vary teaching styles and maintain student interest in the subject. Video provides access to a variety of simulated situations that would not ordinarily be available to the student in the classroom. This can include exposing students to real-life scenarios, experiences and locations which they would not normally be able to access. This simple act of bringing a topic to life and in context is a great motivating factor in education.

Safety and costs

One of the problems of attempting to relate theory to practice in teaching is that it may often involve the risk of exposing students to potentially difficult circumstances, such as safety issues. Examples of such situations may include exposure to dangerous equipment or chemicals in science teaching, or potential health and safety risks, say, on field trips or site visits. Re-creating these scenarios on video can still enable students to experience much of the real situation but from the safety of the classroom.

Another aspect often associated with safety is cost. While it may be possible to take students on visits to demonstrate topics, the associated costs (travel, insurances etc.) often make this unrealistic. In addition, a live demonstration of a method, technique or process may be unrealistic due to the staffing and equipment costs involved. Therefore, if a video of the topic is available at a fraction of the cost, there are advantages to be gained.

Flexibility

The same piece of video clip can be used in different ways to make different points to different audiences. Depending on the level or orientation of the audience, different aspects of the video can be emphasised to make different points, and at differing levels of complexity. This makes the use of video a flexible resource that can be used for a variety of teaching purposes.

Topicality

By using video in the classroom it can help to put content into context and to make it topical. Again, adapting the material based on the audience, video can be made to be topical, depending on their interests, whether these are political, social or cultural. In addition, by using material which is topical, such as current news affairs, it is possible to relate teaching to real life situations.

Stimulation

By its very nature, video can and should be stimulating. One of the main reasons for using video is because it offers unique forms of audio-visual representation that cannot always be represented by other media alone. A well-designed and well-presented video clip can help visualise a concept in a way that text alone cannot describe, or a narrative can clarify complex visual representations.

Accessibility issues

At this point it is appropriate to mention the use of video in relation to the SENDA legislation (see Chapter 1) and, in particular, with respect to partially sighted or blind students. In the case of partially sighted students, video is still a viable educational tool as long as careful thought is given to making it applicable to their particular needs, such as the use of text on screen and avoiding or removing sound effects that might confuse the viewer. With fully blind students, it is still possible for them to benefit from the educational aspects of video by adapting the video with audio transcripts, or with special edits, such as narration, to explain what is happening when there is no dialogue.

The Royal National Institute for the Blind provides a wide range of services, advice and resources on using video for blind students and has produced a booklet on using videos as part of a 'See it Right' pack, which covers a range of issues related to supporting blind people. The Joint Information Systems Committee (JISC) also funds the TechDis service, which aims to improve provision for disabled students. Information on how to access these resources and advice is given at the end of this chapter (see Further Reading).

DEFINING THE QUALITY OF VIDEO

As with any teaching resource, there are well-produced resources and there are poor quality resources, and video is no exception. However, assuming that poor quality video is recognised and rejected by the teacher, it is still possible to turn a good video clip or programme into a poor learning experience.

In order to identify the potential quality of a video, the teacher must first identify a purpose for using it. What is it that attracts the teacher to a particular video clip? Is it the accuracy and presentation of content? Is it the visual appeal that conveys important points across to the audience? It is this sort of questioning that you must address in order to decide whether the clip will be of benefit to the students. It is also at this stage that a good video clip can become a poor teaching aid if you do not explain the purpose of watching it.

Research has long since established that different factors in television production can affect how well people retain information from programmes. For example, information delivered by a narrator is not retained as well if it is accompanied by large amounts of on-screen text. It is up to you, therefore, to be clear about the teaching aims when deciding to use video so that you can convey them to the students. In doing so, the students are better prepared to be attentive to particular aspects of a programme and won't be distracted by miscellaneous information.

From an educational point of view, it has been demonstrated that people who enjoy a 'good' documentary, say, are often only able to recall a few key facts from the entire programme. To make video a more relevant and important learning medium, you therefore have to devise a strategy for focusing students' attention on what is being shown. For example, if you want students to focus on the narrative or pay particular attention to another aspect of the video, this should be clear from the start. There are some standard approaches that can be taken to ensure that video is useful as a learning tool.

THE THREE-PHASE APPROACH TO VIEWING VIDEO

To ensure that students benefit from viewing a good video, or perhaps even to turn a 'poor' video into a valuable learning experience, there is a standard three-phase approach which has proved to be effective:

Phase 1	Play the video.
Phase 2	Replay the video, pausing at appropriate points.
Phase 3	Play the video again.

Phase 1   This phase involves playing the video to give the students an overview of the whole clip and may or may not involve some preparatory work. The students should be told not to attempt to be too analytical at this stage, but rather just to view the clip to get a feel for the content.

Phase 2   It is at this stage that much of the teaching will take place. In conjunction with any preparatory work, such as the use of worksheets, the video should be replayed with pauses at certain points to raise and discuss relevant issues. Depending on the type of activity, you may ask the students to record notes on their worksheets or get them to produce answers based on some preparatory questions. The students could also be engaged in group discussion to comment on the video.

Phase 3   In phase 3 the video is played again to reinforce the points raised in phase 2. This helps students put everything back into context for the whole video clip. To help students' recall of the material, you may wish to pause the video at one or two places but not say anything. This will help students digest the material and reflect on the important issues. Alternatively, you can replay the video in its entirety and allow the students time at the end to reflect on it and perhaps to jot down a few additional notes.

AVOIDING PROBLEMS WHEN USING VIDEO

An ever-present risk when using technology, including a straightforward video player and television, is that things can go wrong in the classroom for a number of reasons. By being aware of these potential mishaps it is possible to plan for them so that even if things don't go as expected, it is still possible to recover the situation and deliver a good teaching session. The following list covers the main problems and explains how to avoid them.

Know how to use the equipment

This may seem an obvious statement, but it is important that the students are given the clear impression that you know how to operate the equip-

 58

Dr Bell quickly got to grips with the video player

ment you are using. Students can become distracted if you waste time trying to set up the video, as they will end up focusing on you more than on the video itself. If you do not familiarise yourself with the equipment, you will also waste valuable teaching time setting things up.

To avoid wasting time and possibly looking foolish in front of the students, you should familiarise yourself with the equipment before the class starts. Ideally, you should visit the room and test the equipment a day or so prior to your class. Alternatively, you should aim to be at least several minutes early for the session to set things up. Also, to reduce the amount of set-up time, you should set the video clip to be at the precise starting point or be aware of the video counter so that you know where to start from. This avoids lost time winding or rewinding a tape as you try to get to the correct part of the clip.

Technical breakdowns

It is everyone's nightmare, but occasionally equipment breaks down in class, which can be a big disincentive for teachers who are considering using technology. However, many apparent breakdowns are really because the equipment has not been set up properly, or occur because a cable or setting has been changed. By taking a bit of time to familiarise yourself with the equipment, in this case a video player, television or data projector (for more information about data projectors, see Chapter 3), you get into the habit of doing standard checks to ensure that the equipment is set up correctly in the first place before you look for technical faults. If you don't feel confident about doing this on your own, there are usually technical staff available within your institution who are more than willing to help you learn how to use the equipment. If you seek help outside of normal teaching activities, there is less pressure on you and you will appear much more confident when using the equipment in front of the students.

Unfortunately, equipment does sometimes break down and there is nothing you can do about it. It is under these circumstances that good planning can make the difference between a wasted teaching session and one which can be salvaged without having to rely on technology. The most obvious preparation is to have back-up equipment available that you can use. Alternatively, it is helpful to know whether you can rely on outside help, such as a technician or porter who can help fix the problem or find replacement equipment. A potential problem with this is the time it may take to find help and rectify the problem, by which time a lot of the session will have been wasted.

Probably a more reliable back-up plan is to prepare alternative activities or teaching materials which you can quickly switch to in the event of technical breakdowns. One obvious solution is to simply carry on with the lecture, using the teaching material that was planned for use after viewing the video. While this may work well, there is a risk that it may not relate to the overall structure because it will no longer be in context now that the video information is missing. Therefore, by pre-preparing alternative activities that cover the video material, it is possible to keep all the content appropriate to that particular session.

Optimal viewing conditions

When showing a video to students, it is important that they are able to view the television or display screen without obstruction. Extraneous light sources, such as daylight coming through a window or an overhead light, can often produce glare on the screen, so preventative steps should be taken to avoid this. The arrangement of the viewing screen in the room can also be a hindrance, so both the students and the equipment should be positioned appropriately. This may mean moving seats around and ensuring that all students have optimal views, even from the back of the room. Another consideration that must be taken into account is ensuring that the students can hear the video properly. Sometimes built-in speakers are not powerful enough and turning the volume up to the maximum produces a distorted sound. This potential problem can be rectified by plugging in external speakers which will give a better quality sound output.

One of the potential problems of using a television to show a video is that you are constrained by the viewing size of the screen, and the equipment itself is bulky and difficult to move between locations. Data projectors, which are audio-visual display equipment, are now available and circumvent these issues (for more detail, see Chapter 3).

TECHNIQUES FOR USING VIDEO IN THE CLASSROOM

There are a number of ways that video can be used in the classroom but they all boil down to ensuring that students can view the material, are able to discuss and record relevant points and are given time to digest the content. From the teacher's point of view the three-phase approach helps meet these requirements, but students must also be given the means with which to achieve this. There are many variations and approaches to this, but essentially they focus on some sort of activity to enable students to take notes and record information, and to discuss the topics being covered. The two approaches concerned are the use of question sheets and debates.

Worksheets

There is a plethora of activities the teacher can use to engage the students, with some examples being given later in this chapter, but many will start with the use of a worksheet of some kind. So that the students are clear about what they are watching and why, providing worksheets helps give a basis for the viewing.

At a basic level the worksheet may simply list a few key questions to prompt the students about certain aspects of the video they should focus on. Questions such as 'What era was the drama set in?' or 'What was the setting for the debate?' give the students pointers as to what to consider. This type of question is a 'closed' question because it requires specific responses. An example of this sort of worksheet is given in

---

Understanding aseptic technique in microbiology

Aseptic technique is the process of ensuring that contamination does not occur during standard microbiological practice in the laboratory. When undertaking microbiological experimentation it is essential to follow certain procedures to avoid contamination by microorganisms from the surrounding environment.

The video you will be shown will demonstrate various aseptic techniques. After viewing the video once you will be asked to answer the following questions. After making an initial attempt at all possible questions you will be shown the video again and can ask questions. The video will then be shown a third time.

How many different methods did you observe?

List each one

Describe the various steps involved in the agar inoculation

Write a short report (no longer than 500 words) on the process of agar inoculation and how the technique avoids microbial contamination through aseptic technique.

FIGURE 5.1 Example of a worksheet with 'closed' questions

Figure 5.1. An open-ended question might ask 'What did you think the character was thinking when . . .'. In this example, the response has no definitive answer and so is 'open-ended'. Figure 5.2 shows a worksheet with open-ended questions.

If the focus of the activity is geared more towards factual recall, a worksheet can be designed to reflect this requirement. For this purpose the sheet would have specific questions asking 'How much?', 'How often?', 'What was the equipment called?', 'Describe the role of . . .', and so on. The design of this sort of worksheet takes more time and effort as you may require single word answers or short passages to be written.

By designing the worksheet in this way, you are giving students prompts as to the type of response expected. For example, if you require a single word answer, you might only leave a small space for writing, but the way the question is phrased may lead students to think they must write more than one word. Therefore, a lot of thought must be given to preparing this type of worksheet. The production of worksheets is also discussed in Chapter 4.

Developing listening skills in language learning

An integral part of developing your oral skills is the development of listening skills. By becoming familiar with Spanish as a spoken language you will be better placed to develop your own oral skills.

Therefore, the purpose of watching the video you will be shown is to listen to the dialogue and to expand your vocabulary. You will not be expected to answer questions in class in Spanish.

The video clip you will be shown is a contemporary drama programme in Spanish. The clip will be shown three times. After viewing for the first time you will be given time to attempt some of the questions listed below.

The video will then be played for a second time with pauses at specific points to discuss the vocabulary and then the video will be played for a third time.

What topic did the discussion focus on?

What were the issues raised by Maria and Pablo?

Why was José angry?

List 5 words used in the scene that best describe the context of the video. In a short report (no more than 500 words) summarise the scene in the video in English, describing the conversations in paraphrase, i.e. do not attempt to recount the content word for word. In addition, list 10–15 words used in the clip which were new to you, providing the English/Spanish translation.

FIGURE 5.2 Example of a worksheet with 'open' questions

Debate

Using video to promote debate among students has many benefits, both in terms of subject content and more general skills development. By encouraging students to discuss the content of a video, you can help develop a number of transferable skills, such as communication and presentation skills. In relation to debating skills directly linked to subject content, students can explore their understanding of a topic and get instant feedback from their peers.

As with the use of worksheets, there are a number of approaches which can be taken, but all of which focus on promoting debate among the students. Probably the most fundamental approach is to play a video and then ask the students to discuss the content. However, this approach is dependent on the dynamics of the group and may backfire if students

---

Debating the issue of Third World debt

With the ever increasing globalisation of business some would argue that there is a greater polarisation of the 'haves' and 'have nots'. One effect of worldwide market forces is that developing countries find themselves in increasing debt to the richer nations, with drastic humanitarian consequences.

In order to avert this crisis and help developing countries become self-sufficient, should Third World debt be abolished?

You will be shown a short current affairs video highlighting the main issues concerning global business and Third World debt. After the clip you will be given a few moments to jot some notes down in relation to the questions listed below.

You will then be split into two groups, one supporting the principle of abolishing debt and the other against it. The video will be played a second time. The rest of the session will then be used to debate whether or not Third World debt should be abolished.

Are bad business practices the sole cause for developing countries getting into debt?

Do businesses offer loans under conditions which borrowers could never hope to pay back?

How did these situations arise in the first place?

Based on the issues raised by the opposing group, how would you solve this problem to most suit your group's interests?

After the debate, produce a short report (no longer than 500 words) summarising the issues raised by both groups, together with a conclusion based on your own arguments.

FIGURE 5.3 Worksheet for promoting student debate

are reluctant to speak. This is a problem often associated with entry level students on a course, where they have little confidence or do not know each other too well and are scared or embarrassed that they might make an inappropriate statement.

To encourage the nature of a debate to focus on specific aspects that you wish to discuss, it is important to provide students with the means to do so. This lead can be provided by a worksheet, as shown in Figure 5.3, offering starter questions for the group to discuss once they have viewed the video. Alternatively, students can be divided into different groups with each group having a different remit, such as one group concentrating on the setting for the video (e.g. epoch, costume, setting) and another looking at the storyline. Both aspects can then be drawn out to consider how perceptions of video relate to each group.

One of the great benefits of debating a video in groups is that students are able to ask questions in a more informal atmosphere, so the learning environment becomes less intimidating. This also provides a good setting

*The debate club was more interactive
than Dr Bell had envisaged*

for peer-supported learning, the benefits of which are well established. However, from the teacher's perspective, chairing a debate takes practice and is a skill which must be developed over time. As with any debate, it can quickly descend into chaos if it is not organised and controlled by you; alternatively, it can become embarrassingly silent if students do not engage in discussion.

When chairing a debate, you must therefore be aware of standard approaches to make the session interactive. If students are reticent, you should have previously prepared questions to try to stimulate debate, or, better still, give these to the students prior to the class and ask them to start the discussion based on their previously prepared comments. At the other end of the spectrum, the debate may become noisy with too many students talking at once. Here, you may have to take the more formal role of a chair and try to ensure that only one person speaks at a time and if the debate is particularly lively, you should make sure that

65

you summarise the main points at the end so that the students remember the important points over the general discussion.

USING VIDEO IN THE DISCIPLINES

It is possible to support student learning for just about all subject areas through the use of video. By its very nature, video has the ability to convey information in ways that other media can never hope to do. Through the dramatisation of literature, video can bring to life characters and cultures, as well as exploring surrounding issues, such as social and political influences. In science, inherently difficult concepts can be visualised more easily and complicated topics can be explained using a variety of animations and examples. Language teaching is another area to exploit the benefits of video through a multitude of ways. Since there are so many possibilities for teaching with video, the following examples list several ways in which video might be used in the classroom in different subjects, all aimed at promoting student learning based on sound teaching methods.

USING VIDEO TO PROMOTE LANGUAGE LEARNING

Purpose

The development of language vocabulary, grammatical comprehension and cultural language idiosyncrasies.

Preparation

Select a video clip from a programme in the given language that shows several characters with different personalities. Produce a list of, say, ten to fifteen adjectives describing character traits that the different characters display (e.g. angry, happy, pensive, considerate). Distribute this list to the students prior to the class and ask them to learn the words in their native language.

During class

- Inform the students that the video clip will show the characters and explain that their actions and mannerisms may be described by at least one or more of the adjectives provided prior to class;

 66

- play the video in its entirety;
- replay the video, pausing at times to point out characters who have demonstrated a particular trait but without stating which one(s);
- give the students a moment to discuss this among themselves before recommencing the video;
- at the end of the clip, ask the students to discuss each of the characters and attribute the appropriate adjectives to each one;
- replay the video without pauses;
- allow time for further discussion to confirm to the students which adjectives were most appropriate for each character and to discuss their actions in relation to your own language, for example, is similar body language demonstrated for particular adjectives such as anger?

Benefits

In this example students expand their vocabulary and grammatical comprehension by putting words into context. By visualising this on video the students are also able to appreciate how language is expressed both verbally and non-verbally.

ENCOURAGING DEBATE IN POLITICS

Purpose

- Development of argument reasoning;
- ability to distinguish fact from conjecture; and
- improvement in factual knowledge relating to a political debate.

Preparation

Select a current affairs debate topic showing two opposing opinions being expressed by opposite ends of the spectrum. Draw out the main topics of discussion and produce several questions based on the political issues concerned. Ask students to research the issues being raised prior to the class.

During class

- Explain that you expect the students to consider how the points raised in the preparatory question sheet are borne out in the debate and to be aware of any additional points discussed which they may not have come across before the class;
- play the video;
- split the students into small groups to discuss the clip and the preparatory questions;
- initiate a debate by asking the students to discuss the contrasting arguments being made and then lead onto the factual basis of these points based on the students' understanding gained from their research;
- play the video again;
- ask the students to produce a report based on the video detailing both sides of the argument, supported (or otherwise) by known facts, and to reflect on the reasoning adopted for such arguments, for example, was an issue raised on factual, political or emotional grounds?

Benefits

Students are able to research the factual background to a given debate, enabling them to distinguish between fact and conjecture. The video also provides the student with examples of how arguments are reasoned out and political approaches adopted to increase the impact on viewer opinion. This helps the student to put political issues into context so as to make more informed and objective judgements on political debates.

IMPROVING CRITICAL REVIEW SKILLS IN SCIENCE

Purpose

- Improve content recall and understanding from fact-based programmes; and
- be able to critique the content objectively.

Preparation

Select a factual programme or documentary based on a topic that the students are studying. Prepare a question sheet which asks the student to list key facts and concepts they already know about the topic in question. In addition, ask the students to list several questions relating to the work, which they would like the answers to.

During class

- Inform the students that they will be shown a video based on the subject in question;
- play the video;
- individually, ask the students to highlight the knowledge they already had that was confirmed by the programme and any questions which the programme answered;
- also ask the students to highlight preconceived knowledge which was contradicted or any questions which were left unanswered by the programme;
- as a group ask the students to list three or four questions which arose as a result of watching the programme but which they perhaps felt were not fully addressed;
- replay the video;
- ask the students to produce a report that details the answers to the questions which were left unanswered by the video.

Benefits

The approach taken with this method is to get the students to evaluate their current level of understanding of a subject. This is done by self-evaluation and reinforcement based on the content provided by the video. By critiquing the programme and the level at which it is able to provide information about the subject, students are able to identify gaps in their knowledge and understanding.

THE USE OF 35 MM SLIDES

The ability to display photographic slides in the classroom has been possible for many years and allows you to visualise many different objects or locations. The standard size and format of a slide is a 35 mm image produced by photographic film.

There are several ways to produce 35 mm slides, but in each case the end result is the production of an image on photographic film. The standard method is simply by taking photographs with a camera and then processing the film; an alternative approach involves the use of computer technology.

Producing 35 mm slides using a standard 35 mm camera

This method of producing slides is achieved simply by using a standard 35 mm camera to take photographs of the object or location the teacher wishes to show in class. Once the photographs have been taken, the film is simply processed and mounted onto slides. The actual processing of the film requires specialist equipment, chemicals and experience, so it is easier for most people to ask a professional film developer to do this for them. Many institutions will have their own photography unit that can offer this service; otherwise, any high street film processor can also undertake this work for you.

Producing 35 mm slides using a film recorder

With the development of computer technology it is also possible to transfer computer (digital) images straight onto 35 mm photographic film using equipment called a film recorder. While not an overly expensive piece of technology (prices start from about £1,000 to £2,000), it is probably something a department or institution might purchase, rather than an individual teacher. Figure 5.4 shows an old Agfa ProColor film recorder, but many film recorders are now available in smaller, desktop sizes. The image is scanned directly onto a standard photographic film and is processed to produce the slide. While the method of producing the slides is still the same, i.e. slides are produced from processing standard photographic film, the fact that the original image is digital offers more options.

Digital cameras are now commonplace, so a film recorder is a relatively easy way to transfer photographs directly onto 35 mm film. It is also possible to turn PowerPoint presentations into 35 mm slides using a film recorder (see Chapter 3).

Film recorder with camera attached for transferring slides onto photographic film

FIGURE 5.4 Photograph of a film recorder connected to a computer

Viewing 35 mm slides

Slides are viewed with a slide projector, of which there are two basic types: one where the slides are stored in a linear compartment, or a more common model, a carousel (shown in Figure 5.5), where the compartments form a circular unit and slides are rotated in sequence.

The bulbs used to produce the projection light are not very powerful, so, in order to see a decent image, the room or lecture theatre usually needs to have most lights switched off or have daylight blocked out to

FIGURE 5.5 A carousel slide projector

leave the room darkened. The only disadvantage of this is that it usually leaves the room too dark for students to take notes.

Using a slide projector in the classroom

As the saying goes, 'A picture can paint a thousand words', so using slides to present images during a class can help enormously. However, a thousand words is also a lot of information, especially if you have a lot of images to show. It is important, therefore, to think carefully about how you present your slides and how many you decide to use during a single session:

- decide which slides to use well in advance;
- make sure they are in a sequence that follows a logical structure for the class;
- produce a crib sheet listing the slide order and brief descriptions as an aide memoire;
- make sure that each slide is visible only in relation to what is being discussed;
- provide a list of all the images you plan to show, with brief descriptions so that the students have a record of the slides.

It is more than likely that you will only have one set of slides to show students. This means that if a student misses your class, say, through

---

Summary of slides from slide show

Slide 1
The shrine of St Thomas in Canterbury Cathedral

Slide 2
The shrine of St John of Bridlington

Slide 3
Slide of re-enactment of English archers, who were successful in attacking the French cavalry during battles in the Hundred Years War

Slide 4
The shield of leopards and lilies associated with medieval and Tudor rulers

Slide 5
Example of medieval church in Norwich

Slide 6
Picture of old building in York, demonstrating densely populated dwellings

Slide 7
Picture of more spacious house, owned by a merchant

FIGURE 5.6 Slide summary list provided for students

illness, they have missed the opportunity to view the slides. Similarly, most people would not, for obvious reasons, be willing to loan them out to students for revision purposes after having viewed them in class. This means that the use of slides can be a limited learning experience if no alternative options are available.

As stated earlier, it may be difficult for students to take notes during a slide show because of the darkened room, so providing students with a list of slides and accompanying descriptions can offer an important revision aid. An example of this is shown in Figure 5.6 The actual slides can still be made available to students if the images are digitised. Even if the slides originated from photographic film, they can be scanned into a computer, i.e. digitised, and, once in a digital format, they can be made available to students at any time. (More information about doing this can be found in the images section of Chapter 8.)

📖 FURTHER READING

Journal of Interactive Media in Education (*JIME*), available online at http://www-jime.open.ac.uk/ (accessed 04/08/03).

See it Right pack (a RNIB publication), http://www.rnib.org.uk/seeitright/ (accessed 30/06/03)

Slater, Paul and Varney-Burch, Sarah (2001) *Multimedia in Language Learning*, London: Centre for Information on Language Teaching and Research.

TechDis, http://www.techdis.ac.uk (accessed 07/01/04).

Chapter 6

Interactive whiteboards

WHAT IS AN INTERACTIVE WHITEBOARD?

A whiteboard is simply a board which teachers and students can write on to make notes or draw illustrations as part of general class work. An interactive whiteboard takes this concept further with the use of computer technology to add text and illustrations, as well as other media to engage students in fully interactive classroom activities. An interactive whiteboard is therefore analogous to a standard whiteboard, but with the ability to incorporate all the features of computer technology to develop media-rich interactive resources to support teaching and learning.

The concept of a whiteboard is one where the teacher or student can produce notes, drawings etc. on the board for everyone to see. Everyone else in the room can view this material and add to it during the lecture or seminar. An interactive whiteboard works in the same way, with two forms being available. The first is an interactive whiteboard tool accessed directly from a computer (discussed as a tool within virtual learning environments in Chapter 8); since this type is accessed through a computer, it is more commonly referred to as an 'electronic whiteboard'. The second type is one that is used in the classroom, which is the focus of this chapter.

WHAT TYPES OF INTERACTIVE WHITEBOARD TECHNOLOGY ARE AVAILABLE?

There are three main types of interactive whiteboard technology:

- electromagnetic;
- resistive membrane;
- infra-red scanners.

Electromagnetic   This type of board consists of a solid state impact-resistant whiteboard which can only be operated with an electronic pen which emits a small magnetic field. The movement of the pen and its magnetic field is picked up by the frame of the board or a grid of wires embedded in the board.

Resistive membrane   These whiteboards consist of a dual membrane resistive board that has a soft, flexible surface. The two layers of resistive material are separated by a small gap which creates a touch-sensitive membrane. The movement of a specialised pen (which won't damage the membrane) is tracked by detecting the pressure of the marker against the surface. However, since the membrane is touch, sensitive, it is just as easy to control actions with a finger or fingertip in place of the pen.

Infra-red scanners   An infra-red whiteboard doesn't rely on the board itself but works on an infra-red beam scanning movement across the board. The infra-red scanner is attached to the side of the board and movement is tracked through the use of special electronic pens which have uniquely encoded 'sheaths' that enable the scanner to detect their position and pen colour.

HOW RELIABLE IS THE TECHNOLOGY?

In terms of durability, the use of a hard surface for electromagnetic and infra-red whiteboards potentially makes them more robust than the soft surface of resistive membrane boards. There is also the issue of tracking; how well the whiteboard is able to track movement and how quickly movement can be translated onto screen displays. There is no real evidence from users that one particular type of whiteboard has proved more robust than another. Therefore, choice of system is probably more dependent on personal choice than reliability as each system is as reliable as the other.

HOW DO INTERACTIVE WHITEBOARDS WORK?

An interactive whiteboard usually requires up to four different components for full functionality: a computer, a whiteboard, a data projector and specialised software. A data projector (see Chapter 3) is not always required, depending on which type of board is used. However, a common

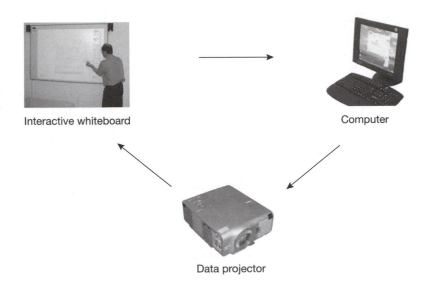

Interactive whiteboard

Computer

Data projector

FIGURE 6.1 A standard set-up for an interactive whiteboard

set-up is one where an interactive whiteboard is connected to a computer with specialised software, in turn connected to a data projector which can display the computer display on the board, as shown in Figure 6.1.

WHAT ARE THE BENEFITS OF USING INTERACTIVE WHITEBOARDS?

- They enable teachers with only basic IT skills to deliver interactive presentations in the classroom. Interactive whiteboards make it easy for teachers to enhance presentation content by easily integrating video/animation, graphics/text and audio.
- The large projected image and special software cater more effectively for visually impaired students and other students with special needs.
- The same features as a traditional whiteboard are provided, such as writing directly on the board, circling things, highlighting or labelling elements on the screen and erasing errors.
- They enable teachers to present student work more publicly.

77

- They allow editing of notes on screen and recording any/all changes or additions, which can be made available to students afterwards.

- They enable students to engage in group discussions by freeing them from individual note taking.

- Students can work collaboratively around a shared task/work area.

- Teachers can easily and rapidly create customised resources from a range of existing content and adapt it to the needs of the class in real time.

- When used for whole class interactive questioning, they can provide student feedback rapidly.

- They support the adoption of e-learning because they demonstrate the potential of alternative modes of content delivery and interaction.

- When fully integrated into a virtual learning environment or other shared content repository, there is a potential for widespread sharing of resources.

A cautionary note about interactive whiteboards

Most, if not all, of the functionality provided by an interactive whiteboard is already available in other forms and may be cheaper than the cost of the interactive whiteboard, for example, presentation tools such as those provided by PowerPoint or applications that include audio and video. However, the big advantage of an interactive whiteboard is that it can bring all these tools together as part of a single system.

The problem of using an interactive whiteboard for only a single use, say, to give presentations, actually defeats the point of purchasing one, since it is just a more expensive way of doing something which can be done by cheaper, alternative methods. Therefore, if you only ever intend to give lecture-style presentations, then the purpose of having an interactive whiteboard becomes redundant. The purposes of using interactive whiteboards are to engage students more fully in a lecture and also to use the various tools to demonstrate topics more interactively.

There are also several logistical issues when considering using interactive whiteboards. Since they are designed to be used in a classroom setting the view can sometimes be obscured towards the rear of the room by people sitting at the front. Also, since the board itself has to be used, it can be difficult for some people to reach the top of the board if they are short or if the board has been placed too high.

Interactive whiteboards can be free-standing or wall-mounted which will also play a part in determining how they are used. Wall-mounted boards may be too high for people to reach, and will also mean their use is restricted to the room in which they are placed. Free-standing ones are more versatile, but their size tends to be limited (usually to about 183 cm, or 72 in) which means that they are more suitable for smaller rooms, rather than larger lecture theatres. Therefore, investing in interactive whiteboard technology must have a clear purpose in order for it to be of benefit.

WHAT PRODUCTS ARE AVAILABLE?

There is a wide range of different products available on the market that covers all three types of interactive whiteboard technology. Anecdotal evidence from users and vendors suggests that the current market share of the products is split roughly evenly as:

	per cent
resistive membrane	35
electromagnetic	35
others	30

There are several models offered by different companies, with a few products using a combination of more than one type of technology. The examples listed below are by no means exhaustive or meant as an endorsement of any particular product. Further product links are cited at the end of the chapter.

Promethean ACTIVBoard

Promethean is a company making an electromagnetic interactive white-board, called ACTIVBoard. Since they are one of the more commonly available types of electromagnetic products, they are also commonly referred to as Promethean boards. The ACTIVBoard can be free-standing or wall-mounted and plugs into a computer, which is connected to a data projector that projects the computer image onto the ACTIVBoard.

In order to use the ACTIVBoard, dedicated software produced by Promethean, called ACTIVStudio, must be installed on the computer. Using a special magnetic pen on the board, it is possible to control the computer rather like using a mouse. The teacher is then able to use the computer to interact with students from the front of the room. It is possible to use most features of ACTIVStudio without being connected to an ACTIVBoard, but the board itself cannot be operated without the ACTIVStudio software.

SMART Board

SMART Board is produced by a company called SMART Technologies and is an example of a resistive membrane interactive whiteboard. Figure 6.2 shows a wall-mounted SMART Board. This type of board operates in a similar fashion to an ACTIVBoard, where the board is connected to a computer and a data projector projects the computer display onto the SMART Board. Dedicated SMART Board software tools also come with the SMART Board, but they will only work if the computer is connected to a SMART Board. However, the SMART Board itself will work with any computer without specific software being installed.

FIGURE 6.2 SMART Board

Mimio

Mimio is a portable capture bar that easily connects to the side of a whiteboard or flip chart. Therefore, Mimio is not strictly an interactive whiteboard product, but one which can turn a standard whiteboard into an interactive one. Mimio technology works through a combination of infra-red and ultrasound. Traditional whiteboard or flip-chart pens can be placed in colour-coded sheaths wired for ultrasonic and infra-red transmission. Pen movement is picked up by the capture bar and can distinguish different colours based on the sheath signal. An electronic eraser can also be used to make corrections or wipe away unwanted material. (See Figures 6.3a and 6.3b.)

It is not essential for a Mimio to be connected to a computer at the same time that it is being used since it can store information within the device. This can then be downloaded to a computer after use. Since real marker pens can be used on a whiteboard or flip chart, students can

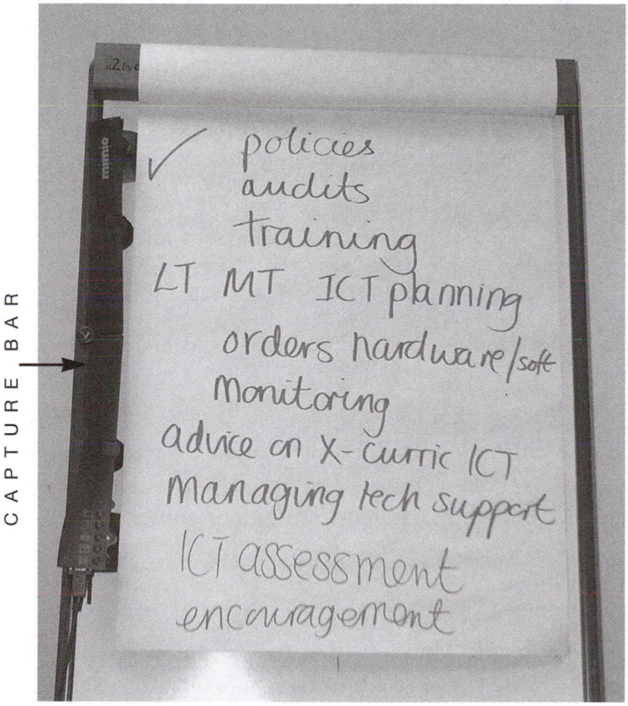

FIGURE 6.3a Mimio attached to a flipchart

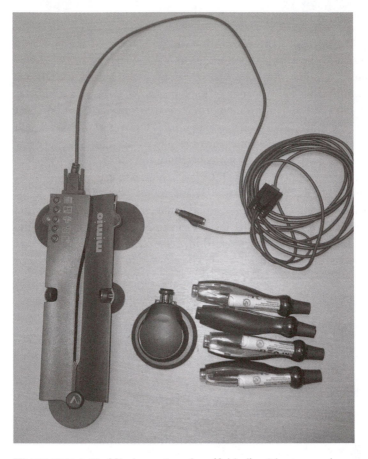

FIGURE 6.3b Mimio capture bar (folded) with pens and eraser

see what is being written without the aid of a data projector. This means that for use in class, only the Mimio and whiteboard are essential. Figures 6.3a and 6.3b show a Mimio capture bar attached to the side of a flip-chart and separately (folded) to demonstrate its portability.

eBeam

This device is similar to the Mimio in that the eBeam attaches to the corner of a whiteboard to make it interactive. It is a triangular device that can be placed on any corner of a whiteboard. Figure 6.4 shows an eBeam transceiver that detects pen movement on a board. An eBeam

■ FIGURE 6.4 eBeam

uses infra-red signal transmission to detect movement from pens, which are placed in signal-emitting sheaths, similar to the Mimio.

Both Mimio and eBeam can operate without having to be physically connected to data projectors, so both can effectively operate as data capture devices from the whiteboard if their full functionality as an interactive whiteboard is not employed.

CleverBOARD

A CleverBOARD (Figure 6.5) combines some of the features of an interactive whiteboard and a Mimio device. The Mimio technology is built into the side of the board (this can be locked for security purposes). If the board is connected to a data projector, the whiteboard can become fully interactive with the aid of an electronic, sheathed pen. Standard software applications can then be accessed with the pen acting as a mouse for point and click purposes.

Wacom tablets and Tablet PCs

Although not strictly interactive whiteboard technology, these devices use touch-screen technology that can be incorporated with data projection to work interactively with students in the classroom. One benefit of this approach is that a data projector can be used in large lecture theatres for interactive computer-based work, rather than smaller-scale whiteboard activities in a classroom.

83 ■

FIGURE 6.5 CleverBOARD

Wacom tablets come in a range of formats and are used widely in the computer graphics industry. They consist of touch-sensitive pads which can be written on and the output is transferred straight to the computer. There are now Wacom products which allow the user to work directly on the screen, so the same principles as used on formal interactive whiteboards apply for drawing, annotating items on the computer screen etc. Tablet PCs work in the same way.

An additional benefit of Wacom tablets is that the pad is available as a wireless device, using infra-red signalling to communicate with a computer. This means that the teacher can pass the pad around the class for students to work on and the rest of the class can see the work projected onto a screen. Again, Tablet PCs can work in a similar way with a wireless keyboard and mouse, which students can use to interact with the PC.

Accessibility

The range of software available for use with interactive whiteboards enables a more flexible approach to supporting students who are partially sighted or fully blind, as well as students with other learning difficulties. For example, most systems are able to magnify the screen display to allow students to view particular parts of the screen more clearly. Handwriting recognition software is commonly available that will turn handwritten notes on the board into editable text. Since this information is quickly transferred from the board to the computer for access to students, screen reader software such as Jaws can be used to 'read' out the text to students. Certain software vendors even claim to be able to convert this text into tactile Braille.

Since it is possible to annotate content on screen and draw ad hoc images to visualise important points, this can be very helpful to students who may have difficulty with text definitions, such as certain dyslexic students. By visualising content in this way, students are better able to grasp concepts and ideas in class. Additionally, enhanced audio options can also help students who are hard of hearing.

INTERACTIVE WHITEBOARD SOFTWARE TOOLS

Staff at the Cascade multimedia training unit, which provides interactive whiteboard training, group interactive whiteboard tools into three basic categories: functionality, generic and speciality (detailed in Table 6.1). Some software tools may be proprietary, i.e. they have been specifically

■ TABLE 6.1 Categories of software tools used for interactive whiteboards

Level	Type	Tools
1	Functionality	Drawing
		Text/graphic editing
		Annotation
		Presentation facilities
		Image capture
2	Generic	Any standard software such as PowerPoint, word processors, spreadsheets
3	Speciality	Handwriting recognition
		Media recording
		Voting
		Resource libraries

designed to work with one product and so cannot be used with different boards. However, software developers are now beginning to design software which will work on any system, so this is becoming less of an issue for users. The tools listed below cover many of the main functions provided by interactive whiteboards, but not all interactive whiteboards will offer all tools.

Functionality tools

Drawing tool   A core tool for any interactive whiteboard is the use of a standard drawing tool. This tool enables you to draw basic shapes such as squares, triangles and so on. There is also the facility to draw freehand with a pen and to use different colours for shapes and lines. Other standard drawing tools include the facility to highlight drawing objects and move things around or erase them.

Annotation images   Many software products provide stock libraries of images and drawings that can be quickly accessed and used. These can include science categories, maps of countries or other unusual geometric shapes. The use of stock images can help save time when trying to describe objects rather than have to draw them from scratch. However, it is also possible to prepare commonly used images and clip art and add them to existing libraries.

Image capture   A common tool for capturing information is an image capture tool that works in much the same way as the 'print screen' button on a standard computer keyboard. The image capture tool can take a snapshot image of the entire board or screen, or allow the user to select just a particular region for image capture.

Presentation tools   At a basic level an interactive whiteboard can be used as a standard presentation tool, similar to PowerPoint. Therefore, there is a range of tools to make presentations more versatile. These include revelation tools, where text or different parts of the board are revealed incrementally so that student attention is focused on specific points. Different resources such as documents, images, audio and video files can be linked together using hyperlink options. Therefore, as part of a presentation a button click might link to some text or an image can be linked to play a video.

Generic tools Interactive whiteboards are capable of mimicking mouse actions, so it is possible to stand at the board and use software, rather than have to sit at a desk in front of the computer. The teacher is able to open programs, click on menus, enter data and carry out other activities that can usually be done sitting in front of a computer. Therefore, any generic software, such as word processors, spreadsheets or other commonly used software, can be operated from the board.

Speciality tools

Handwriting recognition It is possible to turn handwritten notes on the board into editable text that can be copied into other software packages such as a word processor or spreadsheet. There are a number of software applications that offer this functionality and the technology is reasonably robust enough to recognise most people's handwriting. This is a very useful tool for interactive whiteboards as notes can quickly be captured and edited for use by students.

Recording tools Mimio technology allows the teacher to capture all the notes from a whiteboard and download them onto a PC for later use. However, it is also possible with some whiteboards to capture all actions taken, for example, how a particular tool is used or how a complex diagram is gradually developed step by step. Audio can be recorded so the teacher can add a commentary to what they are doing. Recording actions in this way can produce useful multimedia resources for students, which can be replayed as short video clips as part of a teaching and learning activity.

Voting tools Technology for allowing groups of people to vote electronically is now commonplace and a good example is the way television programmes gauge audience responses during entertainment shows or quizzes. The same technology used in a classroom setting has many advantages. Each student is given a hand-held device similar to a remote control unit and enters their vote by pressing the appropriate button (e.g. A, B or C). The infra-red signal from the remote control is picked up by receivers on the interactive whiteboard.

USING AN INTERACTIVE WHITEBOARD

As with any new technology it is important that teachers are confident enough to use interactive whiteboards to support teaching and learning. Rather than expect to be able to use the full range of tools available for an interactive whiteboard right from the start, you can build up experience in stages. There are four basic levels of use:

- presentation;
- annotation and ad hoc examples;
- participation;
- full interactivity.

As experience grows, so the level of interaction can gradually develop from each stage until the whiteboard is being used to its full potential. However, you are not necessarily restricted to slowly developing more interesting uses for whiteboards as it is possible to develop resources prior to a class. Interactive resources with previously prepared content and exercises can be stored on computer and simply accessed when required. This enables you to practise using the different tools and build confidence more quickly. Another big advantage of preparing content is that colleagues can share resources with one another and so build up large resource banks of material.

USING INTERACTIVE WHITEBOARDS IN THE DISCIPLINES

In a similar vein to virtual learning environments (discussed later in Chapter 8), the uses of interactive whiteboards for supporting teaching and learning are almost limitless and can be applied by teachers in any combination of ways. Interactive whiteboards have been used for several years now in primary and secondary education, and as such most examples of effective practice relate to pre-sixteen education. However, further and higher education are increasingly using interactive whiteboards to good effect in a range of subject disciplines.

Using interactive whiteboards in a modern foreign language classroom

An information service, Ferl, which deals with the use of information learning technologies for staff working in post-sixteen education, cites a number of case studies for using interactive whiteboards. One is a 'games box' based on starter, breaker and finisher exercises designed to maintain student interest during a class (developed by Nicholas Mair). By switching the focus or activity, it is possible to maintain student interest and facilitate the learning process. Introducing different language game activities at different times is a good way of switching focus and thus maintaining student attention.

In this context the whiteboard activities are based around EFL (English as a Foreign Language) courses, but can equally be applied to any language teaching of a second language. The games box covers a range of traditional game formats that can be used with the whiteboard. One example is the game 'Blockbusters' where students have to connect two sides of the board by answering questions in the target language, as shown in Figure 6.6. The answer begins with the letter shown in the hexagonal and students use their understanding of the language vocabulary to make a link across the Blockbusters board. The whiteboard can be set up to allow students to interact with the game and by introducing different games at different stages students maintain their interest but also still engage in language learning activities.

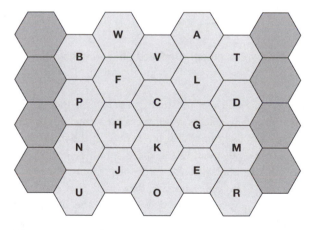

FIGURE 6.6 Screenshot from Blockbusters game on an interactive whiteboard

Creating diagrams to support learning in chemistry

Students at a college in Winchester use interactive whiteboards to improve their understanding of chemistry concepts by producing diagrams of chemical apparatus for experiments. The teacher works with the students to develop an understanding of various chemical reactions in theory, such as balancing equations for a reaction. Based on knowledge about the reaction such as boiling points, the students then have to design an experiment and draw diagrams of how the equipment will operate.

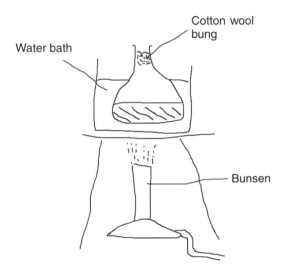

FIGURE 6.7 Laboratory equipment produced on a whiteboard

Students discuss the task in class and then prepare drawings of the experiment. The teacher then selects volunteers to come up to the whiteboard and re-draw the diagram. With the benefit of the interactive whiteboard all the students can quickly see the diagram re-created on a computer screen, which can be saved for future use. Figure 6.7 shows a sample student diagram. The diagrams are then used as a focus for discussion by highlighting any omissions that concern the underlying theory. For example, the reaction may only work at high temperatures and so would need heating first. This should be reflected in the equipment drawn in the diagram.

There are a number of advantages to this approach to teaching and learning:

- the underlying theory is enhanced by group discussions to develop a better understanding of the topic;
- students are able to apply their knowledge to real situations by drawing actual scientific equipment;
- as the diagrams are stored on a computer, they can be used in a variety of ways after the class, including revision aids;
- presenting their work to the class helps students develop their confidence and presentation skills.

While it can sometimes be difficult to get students to volunteer to present their work, one unexpected advantage borne out is that some more able students produce less articulate drawings, which gives other students more confidence to present their own work.

English literature studies supported by multimedia activities

Students studying Shakespeare can often have difficulty in understanding the characters and antiquated dialogue sufficiently well to become fully aware of the story line, together with important historical and cultural references, when simply following written texts. The use of video and audio in a classroom setting helps bring the subject to life by providing additional information and interest not provided by text alone.

There are a number of BBC recordings of Shakespeare's work which can be used free of charge in UK education, provided proper copyright clearance is sought for off-air use. Short excerpts from programmes can be produced, focusing on key speeches or for use as demonstrations highlighting certain historical or even cultural aspects (for example, clothing designs of the period).

It is possible to prepare interactive resources on the whiteboard by linking sections from particular plays and designing group activities around them. The teacher can list particular characters and ask students to discuss what the character says or does, and get them to explore reasons for the character's behaviour. Students can then use the whiteboard to click on the character to hear audio clips and perhaps watch short video clips to provide further interest. Other tools available with a whiteboard allow students to annotate video clips or add comments based on discussions, which can be stored and referenced at a later date.

📖 FURTHER READING

Active Learning in Higher Education Journal, published by SAGE for the Institute for Learning and Teaching in Higher Education (ILTHE), available online at http://www.ilt.ac.uk.

Boud, David, Cohen, Ruth and Sampson, Jane (eds) (2001) *Peer Learning in Higher Education: Learning From and With Each Other*, London: Kogan Page.

CleverBOARD, http://www.cleverboard.com (accessed 09/01/04).

eBeam, http://www.e-beam.com (accessed 07/01/04).

Hitachi Cambridge Board, http://www.interactive-whiteboards.co.uk/hitachi_whiteboards.htm (accessed 18/05/03).

Impulse™ Whiteboard by Polyvision, http://www.westerboards.com/products/ltx.html (accessed 07/01/04).

Mimio, http://www.mimio.com (accessed 07/01/04).

Promethean, http://www.promethean.co.uk.

SMART Board, http://www.smarttech.com/products/smartboard.

wacom, http://www.wacom.com (accessed 07/01/04).

Warren, Chris 'How do Interactive Whiteboards Enhance Learning?', available online at http://www.virtuallearning.org.uk/whiteboards/ (accessed 04/08/03).

Wedgewood IT Group 'Interactive Whiteboards: New Tools, New Pedagogies, New Learning? Some Views From Practitioners', available online at http://www.virtuallearning.org.uk/whiteboards/ (accessed 04/08/03).

Chapter 7

Electronic information resources

Although the paperless office has long been discussed as the way of the future, the reality is that people still use paper and the printed word is far from dead. However, with the globalisation of access to information, more and more resources are now becoming available in electronic format. This brings with it new challenges of searching for information quickly; gone are the days of wandering into a library and browsing through card catalogues.

More and more full-text resources are now becoming available in electronic format, as well as a plethora of other resources, including data banks, image repositories and multimedia resources. Many libraries are now replacing printed resources with electronic resources, not as a way of replacing printed text as such, but for economic or logistical reasons, such as being physically unable to store the ever-increasing range of available publications. In addition, some resources only exist in electronic format, for example, some electronic journals and newsletters do not have a print equivalent.

The outcome of all this is that access to information has increased immensely over the years and it is becoming increasingly difficult to use a library – the traditional source of information within education – without basic C&IT skills. This chapter will review some of the major sources of information services and resources available to (though not always restricted to) UK tertiary education and how to use them appropriately.

Information overload!

WHAT ARE ELECTRONIC INFORMATION RESOURCES?

Electronic information resources come in two basic formats:

Subscription services

The fees for access, usually via the Web, appear high to an individual institution, but on a per capita basis they can work out to be quite cheap. The type and range of services depends on the institution in which you are based, but since there is a subscription charge, the information resource will be quality controlled and reliable. Examples include PsycINFO, a source for Psychological Abstracts and Historical Abstracts for history, related social sciences and humanities subjects. PsycINFO is provided by BIDS (a bibliographic service for the academic community in the UK). Historical Abstracts is provided by a US-based publisher, ABC-CLIO, which has a base in the UK.

Free services

One type of free service is developed and provided by the UK education funding bodies. These resources are quality checked and often peer reviewed, and are available to institutions without subscription. The second type of free service covers a range of web resources which can come from a variety of sources. While these services may be free, there is no quality control and a lot of information is unreliable and of dubious value. SOSIG (Social Science Information Gateway) is an example of a quality-checked, freely-available resource.

THE BENEFITS OF ELECTRONIC INFORMATION RESOURCES

Electronic information resources are inherently beneficial because of their ease of access, which is the reason why there are so many services and resources now available worldwide. The main advantages of accessing and using electronic resources include:

- instant access to a wide range of resources;
- off-campus access for part-time and distance learners;
- tedious and cumbersome manual searching is no longer a barrier to access;
- the increasing demands from students for resources are met;
- access to limited printed resources is less of an issue;
- bibliographic software helps organise and manage references;
- library opening hours cease to matter.

A cautionary note about electronic information resources

One of the disadvantages of accessing and using electronic information resources is the fact that there are so many, which can often lead to confusion. The first big problem is with the use of computer technology to access the services. Many people have a fear of using technology and as a result they are put off by the range of systems that need to be used for accessing the services. There is also the issue of access if certain institutions do not subscribe to some of the services. If they do provide access, there is sometimes a complicated process of password recognition that can cause problems.

The next major issue is that of actually searching through the gargantuan list of resources available. Many students (and sometimes teachers) are ignorant of Boolean operators (see pp. 101 and 168–70) – search options that help to avoid information overload. The result is often unsophisticated search methods where students tend to avoid relevant and specific search tools and go straight for general web search tools such as 'Ask Jeeves' or Google. The results tend to return thousands of 'hits' which are not quality-checked, meaningless and almost impossible to search through.

Another potential problem with electronic information resources is the type of content they provide. Apart from the potential of poor and inaccurate content from free sources, some services have an American bias which may not be in tune with more local requirements. The information available may also be biased if only specific online resources are used, as it is easy for students to 'cut and paste' content. This means that only certain viewpoints are sought because students find it easy to reference only online sources and do not reference other work. Then there are issues surrounding plagiarism due to the wealth of information available and the difficulty of checking authenticity. Therefore, students can present content as their own work due to the difficulty of checking sources of online material.

TYPES OF ELECTRONIC INFORMATION RESOURCES

There are many services and databases available, but the following list provides a reasonable overview of some of the major types of information resources on offer. Although this may appear a daunting list, many of the resources are for specialist use only and the reality is that you are only likely to use several, depending on your requirements. Indeed, you will probably never use certain services as they will relate to disciplines outside your own interests and requirements. For example, a student looking for introductory content on a topic is almost certainly not going to access current research abstracts. As such, you will not need to make students aware of these services.

Common types of information resources cover:

- library catalogues;
- online journals;
- web gateways;

- indexes to theses;
- electronic abstracts and indexes;
- databases of government publications;
- full-text newspapers;
- full-text books (e-books);
- electronic encyclopaedias;
- current awareness alerts;
- education resources such as those sponsored by JISC and LTSN.

For more information about the following electronic resources, please see individual websites.

Library catalogues   There are many different kinds of library catalogues that can be accessed via the Web; these are often known as OPACs – online public access catalogues. The one probably most familiar to you and your students is the catalogue provided by your own institution. This provides access to all the resources available in the institution's library (or libraries) and tells you what resources (books, periodicals etc.) are available and where to locate them.

As well as the local library catalogue, there are also others available such as national libraries for each country (e.g. UK, USA) and specialised libraries that are useful for people researching specific subjects. The UK offers several national catalogues, including the British Library Public Catalogue, which contains millions of bibliographic records. COPAC is another that provides free access to the merged online catalogues of twenty-two of the largest university research libraries in the UK and Ireland, plus the British Library, the national library of the UK.

One of the benefits of OPACs is that they enable students to locate books and journals held in various institutions. Although access is usually limited to staff and students of the host institution, many institutions now offer a reciprocal access and borrowing scheme to provide greater access to resources, such as the RIDING scheme for universities in Yorkshire and Humberside. The benefit to students is that they may gain access to resources in other institutions within their host city, or access local libraries if they travel home during vacation periods.

Athens passwords   Athens is a national system in the UK that enables institutions to provide access to a number of subscribed services through the use of an Athens password. This system only requires a single password and allows students to access a wide range of national and international resources such as online journals. Passwords are provided by individual institutions for their staff and students. However, passwords are only usually required for off-campus access as Athens compares the IP (network) address to confirm authentication from the institution.

Online journals The ability to access and download full-text documents has made the provision of online journals more and more popular. Many publishers now provide access to electronic versions of their journals through electronic journal services such as EBSCO Academic Search Elite (mentioned later in this chapter). This means that a library doesn't physically have to store many journals but can still provide teachers and students with access to content. Increasingly, more and more people are also publishing electronic journals which are not available in paper format. In addition, because electronic publication is cheaper than producing a paper journal and because it is relatively quick to produce materials for the Web, some publishers even provide free access to online journals and periodicals.

Electronic abstracts and indexes Since there are so many journals and other periodicals available, or at least indexed, online there are also services that allow you to search for articles, authors etc. This enables you to locate journal articles and abstracts and their publication of origin. Some of these can be made to show local library holdings. With others you must cross-check with your local library catalogue to find local copies.

Reference management systems (bibliographic software) There are a number of products available which integrate with a word processor to help you organise your references. These reference management systems help you link references to documents and can be used to produce bibliographies. Depending on the product used, you can even search bibliographic databases direct through the software. One example is a product called Endnote in which you can even search databases such as Web of Knowledge for journal articles.

Gateways Gateways, also known as portals, hubs or directories, are collections of information resources on the Web arranged by subject or broad topics. Gateways consist of:

- *General gateways*: this type of gateway provides access to a wide range of web resources which cover educational and recreational content, most of which is not quality-checked or selected on any basis of evaluation. Popular gateways include Yahoo and the Google directory, but another, BUBL LINK, offers access to selected educational resources which are quality-checked.

■ *Subject gateways*: subject-specific gateways provide indexed links that make it easier to search for resources relevant to the subject or topic being researched. Resources contained within subject gateways are sometimes indexed, annotated and evaluated by experts, which means that the content is quality-checked. One example of a subject gateway is PSIgate, a gateway providing resources for the physical sciences community. This is one of many subject gateways on the Resource Discovery Network (RDN) which provides links to resources directly relevant to learning, teaching and research.

Current awareness alerts   Many services, especially those provided by publishers, offer alerts informing you about new publications or periodicals contents lists. These alerts are mostly sent via email. The advantage of this sort of service is that you don't need to keep trawling sites for the latest information about publications. This sort of alert service even extends to other areas such as jobs services. Zetoc is one such service that provides access to the British Library's Electronic Table of Contents of current journals and conference proceedings.

Educational resource services   The UK higher education funding bodies provide a number of information resources. Much of this is done through the Joint Information Systems Committee (JISC) which develops and provides access to a wide range of electronic resources. The JISC is responsible for services such as the Resource Discovery Network and a wide range of publications and links to resources that offer advice about the use of technology-supported teaching and learning.

Another funded body is the Learning and Teaching Support Network (LTSN), which was set up in 2000 to support teaching and learning across all subject disciplines (primarily in higher education) in the UK. There are 24 different subject centres that provide a range of services and resources to support teachers. There are currently proposals to form a new body to support educational institutions, which would build on the work of the LTSN, and is expected to include the title 'Academy'. This Academy is aimed at providing an overarching body that would offer resources, advice and links to information of direct relevance to teachers in all subject areas.

Getting help

One half of the battle for teachers and students is knowing what information resources exist and what they can use. The other half is understanding how to search through the vast amount of information available to locate specific resources of interest. Many teachers make the mistake of thinking that students will somehow know how to find these resources, have the necessary C&IT skills to use them and know how to search effectively for such resources. It is essential, however, that you provide students with all the help they need to carry out searches for information resources.

The first step is to ensure that students have the necessary computing skills. Although younger students tend to have most computer skills needed to undertake information searches, many mature students or international students do not. In addition, there are several key skills which students need to learn to search effectively. These days, most institutions have experienced and well-trained library services or other pertinent staff who provide structured training for students (and teachers) to enable them to use information resources effectively. Many of these staff are also able to put these skills into the context of the subject being taught. Therefore, if you expect students to be able to locate and use information resources as part of their study, you must provide them with the skills to do so.

SEARCHING FOR ELECTRONIC INFORMATION RESOURCES

Many institutions now provide a range of programmes that provide help and training for students to search for online information resources. With the development of virtual learning environments (Chapter 8) this support is often available online too. Work undertaken by David Pennie, Katy Barnett and the author describes one such programme, where students are able to develop their skills alongside their studying, putting the skills development into context. This work covers seven key steps:

1   identify what you want;
2   define your topic;

3   find books on your topic;
4   find periodical articles on your topic;
5   get hold of the material;
6   find World Wide Web resources;
7   record what you find.

As part of this work students are given some key tips on searching, such as:

Select a language   If English is your preferred language, you can narrow the search and reduce the number of 'hits' by selecting only English texts (or any other language, depending on your choice).

Use Boolean operators   In addition to typing general keywords it is possible to refine your search using Boolean operators (and, or, not) to produce more specific searches. For example, if you were looking for information about the geographic term 'oasis' you may search for 'oasis and desert' or 'oasis not music' to avoid finding information about the music band, Oasis. (See pp. 168–70 for more information about Boolean operators.)

Keyword search   When doing a keyword search, it is important to be as specific as possible, otherwise you may produce too many 'hits', i.e. sources of information. Terms such as 'biology' or 'Shakespeare' are too general if you are looking for a specific aspect of biology or information about a specific Shakespearian play. You are more likely to find what you are looking for if you are able to use more than one keyword relevant to your search.

Authors   One way to find relevant information is to do a search on specific authors. If you are aware of an author who has written resources or information that are relevant to you, then doing a search for that author may reveal other related work.

EXAMPLES FROM THE DISCIPLINES

Web of Knowledge

Despite its name, Web of Knowledge (WoK) offers subscription access to a range of multidisciplinary databases of high quality research information from the world's leading science, social sciences, and arts and humanities journals. Access in the UK is via Athens authentication, which will be provided by subscribing institutions. One of the advantages of WoK is that all references accessed can be downloaded and imported into reference management systems.

EBSCO Academic Search Elite

EBSCO Information Services provide a range of resources, including subscription to full-text and bibliographic databases. Academic Search Elite is one of the services provided by EBSCO that offers a variety of proprietary full-text databases and popular databases from leading information providers. Figure 7.1 shows the initial search page for Academic Search Elite.

This multidisciplinary database offers full text for nearly 1,850 scholarly journals, including more than 1,250 peer-reviewed titles. It offers information in nearly every area of academic study, including: social sciences, humanities, education, computer sciences, engineering, physical sciences, language and linguistics, arts and literature, medical

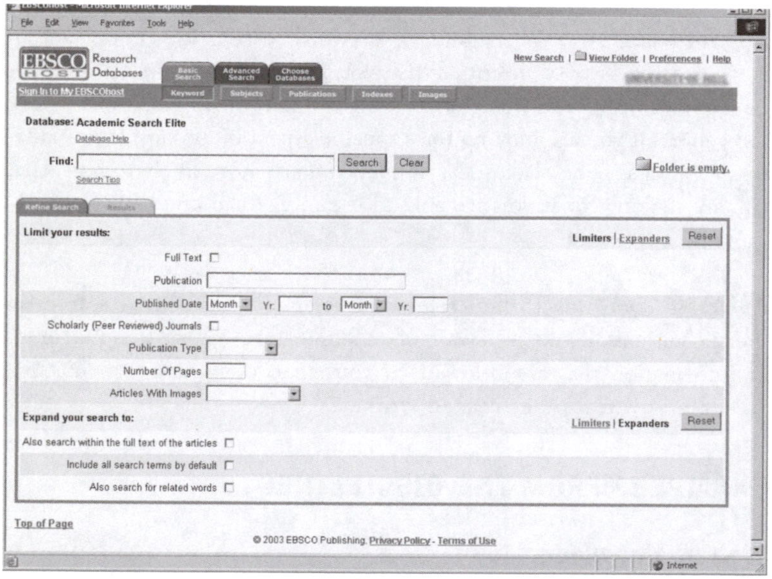

FIGURE 7.1 A screenshot from the initial search page of EBSCO Academic Search Elite

sciences, ethnic studies and more. In addition to full-text publications, indexing and abstracts are also provided for all 3,250 journals in the collection.

Engineering

One example, taken from the University of Hull, where students are provided with training to develop skills in finding electronic information resources, is an engineering module on professional skills. This is run for level three undergraduates on a four-year course. There are two main aims: to give students practical help in finding resources for their final year dissertation and to give a wider view of the professional skill of finding information, the process and problems, which they will need as professional engineers.

The course involves introducing the students to:

- the Library catalogue;
- the subject-specific database 'Compendex' and the multi-disciplinary database and citation index 'Web of Knowledge' to track down article references;
- full-text electronic journal databases such as EBSCO; and
- quality-controlled subject gateways such as EEVL, the Internet Guide to Engineering, Mathematics and Computing.

Also covered are the advantages and disadvantages of electronic information, e.g. fast, flexible, ease of recording, full-text databases and the risk of information overload, access issues, plagiarism and so on.

A task is set asking students to answer various questions about the process of information gathering and they are also given a practical exercise searching an electronic index and recording what they find in correct referencing style.

Research skills for forensic science

Dr John Wheeler at the University of Staffordshire runs a level two core module for all forensic science students with the clear aim 'To develop skills in carrying out research work'. The module covers literature (searching and reporting), research (proposing, planning, executing and reporting) and critical reflection.

During the module the students choose a topic of 'current' interest in forensic science, perhaps relating to a new fingerprinting method or work relating to a current criminal investigation. Based on their own choice, the students then research the topic and produce a review paper summarising the work. The students have to reflect on and critically evaluate all activity throughout in a 'learning diary'. This approach helps give a subject-focus to developing information search skills.

This module helps students to improve their abilities to critically review research and to produce meaningful reports. The assessment is based on a review paper, a mini research project and the learning diary. There is a poster session at the end of the module where the students present their work. Among the many skills developed during the module, including independent learning and reflection and critical evaluation, the students are able to apply their skills to researching their final year projects.

FURTHER READING

BUBL LINK, 'Study Skills', available online at http://bubl.ac.uk/link/s/studyskills.htm (accessed 04/08/03).

Compendex, http://www.engineeringvillage2.org (accessed 07/01/04).

EEVL, http://www.eevl.ac.uk.

Owen, Tim (2000) *Success at the Enquiry Desk: Successful Enquiry Answering – Every Time*, 3rd edn, London: Library Association.

Psigate, http://www.psigate.ac.uk/newsite.

Resource Discovery Network (RDN), http://www.rdn.ac.uk.

SOSIG, http://www.sosig.ac.uk (accessed 07/01/04).

Yahoo, http://www.yahoo.com.

Chapter 8

Virtual learning environments

Over the years computer technologies have been developed to support teaching, such as assessment or communication tools. In more recent years, technology developments have enabled these tools to be combined into single products, called virtual learning environments, or VLEs. Therefore, a VLE can be defined as a self-contained computer-based (web) environment enabling interactions between teacher and student.

Unfortunately, as with all computer-related technologies, there is usually some confusion with terminology and VLEs are no different, with the term MLE (managed learning environment) often being used interchangeably with VLE. A VLE handles information directly related to student teaching, for example, lecture notes, online discussions and perhaps student grades. In addition, an MLE deals with the management of other information which may not be directly connected with teaching 'in the classroom'. This information could include student personal details and information such as module or financial information. Therefore, a VLE is really a subset of the information contained within an MLE. So, although a VLE can cover a lot of what an MLE offers, and is the important component in direct teaching activities, an MLE can offer much more in the way of information management.

Certain products available on the market are capable of acting as both a VLE (purely teaching support) and an MLE (integrated information management), so an MLE might be employed to operate in the same way as a VLE but would still have the additional functionality of an MLE if required, hence the interchangeable terminology. For the purpose of this chapter, the term VLE is used since the focus is on direct teaching support, rather than the more complex issue of total student information management within an MLE.

Having put all this terminology into context, this chapter will now focus on the use of VLEs and how they can be used to support teaching, rather than simply how to use the technology. In this book there is also a separate chapter on e-learning, which the reader might initially think overlaps with what is covered in this chapter. However, VLEs provide the platform on which e-learning takes place (the tools) and e-learning itself provides the methodology (the skills) to support effective teaching and learning practice.

MANAGED LEARNING ENVIRONMENTS

Although this chapter focuses on the features of a VLE in direct relation to teaching and learning, it is worth briefly mentioning the reason for the evolution of MLEs, since their impact on education is likely to grow. If you consider students within an institution, there is a lot of information which is connected with them, ranging from personal details (addresses, qualifications, etc.) to exam results and module choices. Much of this information is held by different people and in different databases.

It is essential that this information is accurate, not duplicated, and accessible by relevant people (including the student) in a quick and reliable way. Therefore, the management of this information is very important. Figure 8.1 visualises the way different resources and information sources can link together in an MLE.

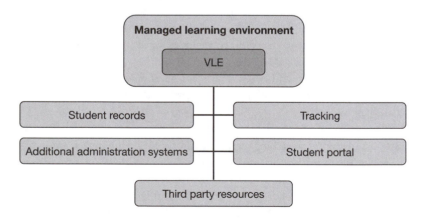

FIGURE 8.1 An MLE encompasses a VLE and provides links to other systems

In a learning support context, students can be provided with resources specific to their own course or module, or have access to customised external resources such as journal archives or scientific data sets. Technological developments already allow (to a large degree) students to log in to an MLE and have customised access to their own records, teaching material and even more extraneous information such as news or weather reports, and may even allow them to pay fees online. This means that teachers are increasingly able to provide students with access to a wide range of customised electronic resources to support individual learning needs.

WHAT IS A VIRTUAL LEARNING ENVIRONMENT (VLE)?

A VLE is an online (web) environment, where various tools are provided for the teacher and the student to facilitate the learning experience. VLEs generally operate across the World Wide Web, so you often only need an Internet connection to access a VLE, although access will be restricted to registered students by the teacher. Figure 8.2 illustrates the core features of a VLE.

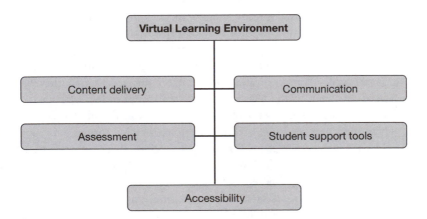

FIGURE 8.2 VLE offers wide-ranging functionality

WHAT ARE THE BENEFITS OF USING A VLE?

If we now consider the case for using VLEs to support teaching and learning, it is useful to consider what face-to-face teaching can offer in order to foster learning:

- information delivery;
- peer support;
- group work;
- self-assessment;
- formative/summative assessment;
- teacher–student communication;
- tutorials.

A VLE provides a range of tools to facilitate the same teaching and learning principles, but they are delivered online in a 'virtual' environment. Thus, using computer technology does not involve a whole new approach to teaching; it utilises the same methods but applied in a different way. However, this means that the same thought and consideration must also be applied to online teaching as you would do with face-to-face teaching.

To take a fundamental example, many lecturers now transfer their lecture notes to the Web. The outcome of this is that printing costs are transferred to the students and many expect it. Indeed, many institutions even provide students with prepaid print quotas to offset some of these costs. There is nothing inherently wrong with this, but the lecturer must consider how the students are going to use these notes. Are the students expected to read and comment on the notes? Will they be assessed on them? If the lecturer has no real purpose for offering the notes, then what is the point of giving them out in the first place?

It is important to realise here that exactly the same sort of questions apply equally whether the information is paper- or computer-based, hence the teaching method is more important than the technology. Therefore, technology should not be used for the sake of using technology but with a specific teaching and learning purpose in mind.

In addition to supplementing traditional face-to-face teaching methods, there are a number of challenges in education which VLEs can help with and these include:

- increased student numbers;
- increasing assessment marking;

■ widening participation;
■ limited teaching resources.

The reason VLEs have become so popular and embedded in many institutions is because there are real benefits to be gained from the use of the technology. Ever-increasing student numbers is one obvious issue for institutions where VLEs can help. They can maintain good communications links and there are opportunities for automated assessment. In terms of widening participation, VLEs can provide support and resources to, say, part-time students who can't always travel to the campus.

WHAT PRODUCTS ARE AVAILABLE?

There is a plethora of commercially produced and home-grown products available, probably too numerous to mention here. The following list of products is therefore just a sample of commonly used products or current market leaders in either further education and/or higher education, in no particular order.

COSE   Developed at Staffordshire University around sound pedagogical theory, this product is free.

http://www.staffs.ac.uk/COSE/

Learnwise
This was originally developed at the University of Wolverhampton and is now marketed as a commercial product by the Granada Learning Group.

http://www.learnwise.com/

Blackboard
Blackboard is an American company that started in 1997 and is now one of the larger vendors of commercially developed MLEs (Figure 8.3). It offers different levels of functionality, depending on the type of licence purchased.

http://www.blackboard.com

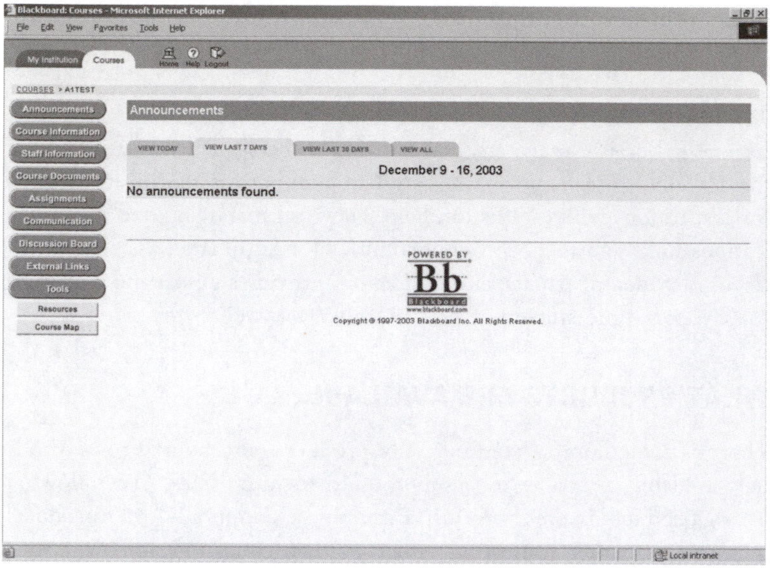

FIGURE 8.3 A screenshot of a Blackboard course

FIGURE 8.4 A screenshot from a WebCT course (image taken from WebCT course demonstrated on WebCT's web site)

WebCT   WebCT is another market leader of MLEs and, together with Blackboard, is arguably one of the main commercial vendors to UK educational institutions (Figure 8.4).

http://www.webct.com

WHAT TOOLS CAN A VLE OFFER?

Communication tools

It is obvious that communication between students is a valuable source of interaction, enabling them to discuss new ideas and share information. It is very difficult to single out a specific method of using communication in teaching because there are so many ways to communicate. At a very base level it can be used as supplementary support to keep students informed about day-to-day activities, such as work deadlines or timetable changes. Using a VLE as a communications tool in this way quickly adds to the teaching support role which students might otherwise miss.

Email   Electronic mail (email) is now a familiar form of communication for most people, and any worthwhile VLE should have some sort of email communication tool.

Discussion boards   Another fundamental tool is that of a discussion board. This is analogous to a physical notice board on the wall in a department, where anyone can post a message for everyone else to read and anyone can respond to this message on the same board. An electronic notice (or discussion) board works in much the same way by allowing people to post messages for other people to read and to post replies. One benefit of this is that group discussion can be encouraged.

Electronic discussion boards enable two-way dialogue between teacher and student, or student and student. One benefit of this is to promote problem-solving skills. Solving problems involves students articulating and sharing ideas and getting feedback on problems in order to develop a strategy for solving the tasks and working towards an answer. By providing a communication forum with which to facilitate this process, it is possible to get a better understanding of how students work through these problems and provide useful feedback as and when required.

Live chat   This tool allows synchronous communication (i.e. at the same time) and sometimes is referred to in different ways, often called 'chat rooms' by commercial providers with which many people are familiar. One benefit of this tool is that it can enable students to communicate even if they are in different locations. Although the same is true of discussion boards, the communication is immediate due to students chatting synchronously.

Another advantage of communication tools is the ability to archive (store) discussions which can be used as resources for future students. For example, a useful discussion might develop around a particular topic which may be historically difficult for students to conceptualise. Through discussions involving yourself and students, a successful summary of the issues surrounding the topic might arise. This may then be helpful to future students in helping them understand the topic.

Content delivery

A core tool of any VLE is the ability to deliver content in a variety of formats. This can consist of delivering: lecture support notes; presentation files; images; or even audio or video material; as well as interactive animations.

Lecture support notes   Delivering lecture support notes can be a useful aid for teaching and learning. Lecture notes available via a VLE can be accessed by students at any time and this can be of great help to them. Student learning becomes much more flexible since it provides resources at a time that suits them and doesn't restrict content delivery to the classroom.

There is the argument that if students are given the lecture notes prior to a lecture, they will not turn up for the lecture. To avoid this problem and to make more use of the lecture time, students can be given a set of skeleton notes, i.e. with sections or points omitted. There are two advantages to this approach: first, students have to attend the lecture to gain a full set of notes; and second, since students only have to note down a few key points, more time is available for discussing topics with you during the lecture.

Images   The use of images in teaching can greatly help visualise concepts or descriptions of objects, locations, art etc. For example,

■ **FIGURE 8.5** Image of liquid crystals (reproduced by kind permission of Prof. John Goodby, University of Hull)

offering slide shows during lectures can present many different images to the students. This helps bring a lecture to life and to stimulate interest; although a disadvantage is that the students don't have access to your set of slides afterwards, for example, if they were ill and missed the lecture.

It is now very easy to digitise (scan) images and make them available on a VLE, allowing for copyright of course. (The same copyright law exists for electronic information as with any other medium, so you should seek advice from your institution if you are not sure about the use of any third-party content.) Through the simple act of making such images available, it is possible to make content more interesting and also give students access to images which they can also use as aide memoires. One such example is the visualisation of liquid crystals, as shown in Figure 8.5. Due to the abstract nature of the crystal images, students can benefit greatly from being able to reference the images at any time.

Electronic whiteboards

If you consider the use of a whiteboard in a physical class setting, you can write notes on the board and ask students to contribute, with the other students able to view the work. Applying the same principle to a VLE tool, students are able to compose materials interactively in a synchronous way where everyone sees the work from their own computer and is able to contribute. Again, an advantage of this is that you can work with the students, without having to be located physically in the same place.

In addition to the type of electronic whiteboard facility available as a VLE tool, there is also another type, which is a classroom audio-visual aid. This type of whiteboard is discussed in detail in Chapter 6 and is referred to as an interactive whiteboard.

Assessment

Many VLEs offer computer-assisted assessment tools that enable you to assess students online. Although not all VLEs are capable of offering assessment tools, there is a wide range of independent assessment products available which can sometimes be linked to a VLE to enhance its functionality.

There are well-established methods of assessment and much research has been undertaken about the validity of different types of assessment, such as the ability of multiple-choice quizzes to assess deep (comprehension) or surface level (factual recall) learning. These questions apply equally to paper-based assessment and computer-assisted assessment within a VLE. Therefore, computer-assisted assessment is no less valid than paper-based assessment and has an important role to play in supporting teaching and learning.

The range of assessment options available usually includes: multiple choice questions; true/false answers; fill in the blank; ordering or matching questions (e.g. list or image labelling); and typed response questions (open content) – though this question format cannot be marked automatically by the VLE. Each has its own strengths and weaknesses, but some of the main advantages of electronic assessment are instant marking, quick data analysis and quick feedback for students. An example of how computer-assisted assessment is used in teaching and learning is given towards the end of Chapter 9 on e-learning.

There are wide-ranging issues concerning computer-assisted assessment, too numerous to mention in the context of this book. Therefore, several good starting points for further reading about computer-assisted assessment are given at the end of the chapter.

File exchange and group work

Over and above the ability for staff to provide students with files, students are also able to share files with one another. This means that students are able to share work in an online environment rather than have to meet face-to-face all the time. A student could potentially share resources with fellow students or put work up for comment. Taking this into account with the other tools available within a VLE, students can therefore communicate with each other, share ideas and files online and collaborate on work as part of a group.

Miscellaneous tools

Depending on which VLE you use, there may be additional tools available. Some of the more common ones include online calendars and task lists where you and students can post entries. This functionality helps students to plan their work and activities in much the same way that

TABLE 8.1 List of core VLE tools

Category	Tool
Communication	Email
	Discussion board
	Live chat
Content delivery	Lecture support notes
	Images
	Audio
	Video
	PowerPoint presentations
Assessment	Assessment tools
	Online grades
Miscellaneous	Interactive whiteboards
	File exchange
	Calendar and task lists

people use electronic personal organisers. Some VLEs also offer tools to check grades so that students can review past assessment marks. The more commonly available VLE tools are listed in Table 8.1.

EVALUATION

In addition to computer-assisted assessment, similar tools can often be used to deliver anonymous surveys. An advantage here is that electronic surveys can be administered to students and the results analysed quickly. Perhaps an obvious primary use is to use this tool to obtain evaluation data from students.

However, one of the major problems with VLEs is that evaluation is often an afterthought when it should actually be one of your first considerations. When deciding to use a VLE to support teaching and learning, you should have a clear idea of what it is you hope to achieve. You may want to consider the role of communication tools and their effect on promoting student collaboration and peer support. The evaluation should then be prepared so that it will elicit the relevant data to support your aims, based on a set of relevant and valid questions that will provide explicit responses. Evaluating the effectiveness of VLEs and the wider role of e-learning is discussed in more detail in Chapter 9. The wider issue of evaluating C&IT use in teaching and learning is also the focus of Chapter 12.

ACCESSIBILITY

When mentioning accessibility, many people might automatically think about support for disabled students and how technology might help them. Although this is a pertinent point and there is certainly a wide range of support technology available, there is also the assumption that everyone has access to a networked computer off-campus and hence access to VLEs. The issue, therefore, is not just one of accessibility but of fair access for everyone.

Technology can improve access to resources for disabled students and it is important to be aware of the SENDA legislation that came into force in September 2002, making educational institutions more accountable for supporting disabled students. This legislation is covered in Chapter 1. For example, a blind student can use screen reader software to 'read' content. But what if the content has been developed without consideration for a blind student? If a student is asked to describe a colour, how would a blind student describe that colour if they do not understand the concept of colour in the same way as a sighted person? In this way, thought would therefore need to be given to developing content in such a way that it does not unfairly disadvantage some students.

In terms of fair access, it is easy to make the assumption that all students have use of a networked computer at home and can therefore access a VLE at most times during the week. If students are expected to use a VLE as part of the module, if they didn't have Internet access at home, they would be at a disadvantage in relation to other students. One solution is to gauge how many hours you expect students to use the VLE during the week and make computer facilities available on campus for comparable hours. Many institutions now have computer facilities which are open long hours or even provide 24-hour access for students.

ISSUES TO CONSIDER WHEN USING A VLE

Since VLEs offer so much functionality, it is easy to become overwhelmed by them and what they can offer in terms of teaching and learning support. Therefore, the most important starting point is to consider how the technology can help support your teaching and not how your teaching can fit the technology. By considering the following points, the integration of VLEs into your teaching will be more successful:

- have a clear purpose in mind for using VLEs;
- have a clear plan for using a VLE to support your teaching;
- get used to using the technology before introducing the students to it;
- give students time to get used to using it;
- make sure the students understand why they are using it and what the benefits will be.

The range of tools listed may vary between VLE products, with some offering some tools but not others, or some tools being more versatile between VLEs. As you might expect, the teaching and learning possibilities are almost endless, given the range of tools available, and it is simply down to you, the teacher, how you use the tools to support your teaching and learning activities.

USING VLES IN THE DISCIPLINES

Peer support for student nurses

Due to ever-increasing student numbers, teachers often have to deal with larger classes. This means less time for personal tuition and many students often end up working in informal groups during and after class to support each other. This is not necessarily a bad thing, as it offers the opportunity for peer support; you can also organise more formal group work exercises.

However, it may be difficult for a group to meet up to discuss their work and coordinate activities. In the case of nursing students, many tend to be mature students, i.e. outside the traditional 18–21 age bracket, and they often have commitments over and above study, such as work placements or other outside obligations. Students may have timetable clashes due to differing module choices. Some students may not live near the campus and so cannot easily come into the institution outside of formal teaching hours.

By employing a VLE, it is possible for the nurses to communicate with each other and yourself electronically. It is also possible to share work and exchange notes. You can provide online exercises and any group questions can be coordinated through a spokesperson, so you can address the whole group. There is also the facility to submit electronically draft documents and even the final completed work.

In adopting such approaches to support learning, although students may have a disadvantage in that they occasionally work in isolation, they will be more confident knowing that there is a formal system of support, communication and access to resources which otherwise would be denied them because of logistical constraints. From the teacher's point of view, group activities can continue outside normal teaching hours and a peer system develops which fosters a better teaching and learning environment.

Group work

Group work ties in closely with peer support and simulation work. As with face-to-face group work, where students collaborate together and periodically liaise with the teacher, VLE-supported group work can act in much the same way. One of the advantages of supporting group work in this way is that student progress can be monitored more closely, as well as allowing you to offer more timely support. Many VLEs offer miscellaneous tools such as online calendars, task lists and reminders that enable both you and the students to coordinate deadlines.

This sort of activity is not restricted to any one discipline, but must be well organised if it is to add value to teaching and learning. The group activity should be broad enough to provide adequate input from all members of the group, but not so broad that students feel overwhelmed. Therefore, clear guidelines must be given about what is to be expected in terms of deliverable work. The dynamics of the group must also be taken into consideration, depending on whether the students are level one, say, or final year students. This can have a big impact on how well a group operates, for example, level one students will often need more guidance on how to share tasks. Therefore, they may need help on how to divide the workload, such as nominating a group spokesperson.

By coordinating the group work through a VLE, it is possible to keep a record of how the students are progressing. Records can be kept of how often students communicate online and you can offer support at appropriate times if students are struggling to complete the tasks. Overall, many students enjoy online group activities for various reasons, not least because it helps deepen their understanding of the subject, but also because they receive recognition for their contribution to the group activities in an online environment.

Simulation work and problem-based learning in chemistry

Over the years, computer simulations and problem-based learning have developed to help students simulate a range of practical activities which would otherwise be costly in terms of time, space or even on safety grounds. Although there is often no substitute for the real activity, simulations can help the student address and answer many of the same problems posed in the real-life situation. Another benefit is that the activity is not restricted to formal teaching hours, where students may only have a morning and/or an afternoon to work with you. Therefore, the use of VLEs to promote this work can be combined with existing classroom activity.

One way of promoting problem-based learning for chemistry students within a VLE is to devise an experiment where the students are given certain information to start with. This online activity helps students prepare for a real laboratory session, where they only get one chance to undertake the practical work. If the experiment doesn't work for any reason or they fail to record appropriate results, the learning experience may be diminished.

For the problem-based learning approach, after being given the initial information, students have to do tasks based on prior knowledge about the subject to postulate outcomes. As they continue working, they are then given bits of data or clues to help them until they reach a conclusion about the objectives of the experiment, what underpinning chemistry is being tested and what type of outcomes they might expect. After this 'pre-lab' preparation, the students are able to undertake the real experiment with more confidence, understand the principles behind the work and obtain more meaningful results to analyse.

Simulations can be used in much the same way for mimicking other scenarios. However, simulations are often more appropriate for situations where the real experience may be unfeasible due to logistical reasons such as cost, safety or time constraints. The benefit here, however, is that the outcomes can be more open-ended, which provides more scope for student exploration of a topic. Although simulations can be run within a VLE, such as simulated voting in the politics example in Chapter 9 or laboratory simulations in Chapter 11, there is a plethora of self-contained simulation resources freely available for a wide range of subject disciplines. The Learning and Teaching Support Network (LTSN) is a very good starting point for locating these resources. Although such simulations are not run directly through a VLE, it is possible to design activities in such as way as to promote additional problem-solving work or group work within a VLE, as discussed earlier.

FURTHER READING

Brown, Sally, Bull, Joanna and Race, Phil (1999) *Computer-assisted Assessment in Higher Education*, London: Kogan Page.

Bull, Joanna and McKenna, Colleen (2003) *Blueprint for Computer-assisted Assessment*, London: RoutledgeFalmer.

Maier, Pat and Warren, Adam (2002) *Integrating Technology in Teaching and Learning: A Practical Guide for Educators*, London: Kogan Page.

Salmon, Gilly (2000) *E-moderating: The Key to Online Teaching and Learning*, London: Kogan Page.

Virtual Learning Environments (Becta ICT Research), available online at http://www.becta.org.uk/research/reports/vle.cfm (accessed 04/08/03).

Chapter 9

E-learning

THE EVOLUTION OF E-LEARNING

Back in the 1980s and 1990s, computer technology began to develop and expand quite rapidly beyond just the relative confines of the large, corporate mainframe users. This expansion, partly due to the falling cost of the technology, meant that the general public could start purchasing personal computers. The Sinclair ZX Spectrum, for example, with its 48Kb of memory was a huge commercial hit. This meant that teachers were also increasingly able to purchase the technology and use it to develop teaching resources for their students.

Government support for developing and disseminating resources became available, such as that provided by the Computers in Teaching Initiative (CTI) centres and the Teaching and Learning Technology Programme (TLTP). As a result, lots of resources sprang up which enabled students to learn from a variety of software for a wide range of subject areas. Much of the content in these software packages was designed to act as supplementary material linked to face-to-face teaching, or as an optional 'bolt-on' to the course, but rarely as an integral part of the course.

Several terms grew to describe this approach to teaching support, commonly referred to as Computer Assisted (or Aided) Learning (CAL), Computer Based Learning (CBL), or even Computer Based Training (CBT). Whatever the term used, one thing they all had in common was that these resources developed before the advent of the Web and so, for a student to access the material, they often had to have direct access to the software on a stand-alone computer. With few students owning their own PC, this also meant competition among students for access to limited resources within their institution.

Dr Bell took delivery of the new compact version of the X300 home computer

Much of the content this software provided was limited in scope and much was poorly designed, being little more than electronic textbooks that added little to the learning experience. With the development of the Web and the range of technologies that surround it, such as better content management, digital video technology and animations, the potential for interactive learning increased dramatically.

Moving forward to the present day, students are now able to access a wide range of learning resources via the Web that offer interactive content and communication facilities. The starkest contrast between the old style CAL and e-learning is that it has become less instructional, focusing less on teaching and more on learning. In addition, the Web has stretched e-learning beyond the boundaries of the classroom or dedicated computer teaching room, offering many more opportunities for students in terms of access.

WHAT IS E-LEARNING?

Now that technology has enabled us to expand teaching and learning beyond the confines of the classroom, students are able to access resources in different ways and at different times. In actual fact, students studying on distance taught courses – at the Open University, for example – have engaged in this approach for many years but without much of the technology until recently. In doing so, open and distance learning (ODL) courses have had to develop sound teaching methods, or pedagogies, to ensure that the learning experience for the student is a valuable one.

E-learning has a lot of similarities with ODL in that it delivers teaching and learning resources to students at a distance (even if it is just across the campus) but is focused primarily on the use of technology. Therefore, e-learning can be defined as the delivery of technology-supported teaching and learning, based on sound pedagogical teaching practices. This means that e-learning is not a passive medium for delivering content, but is an interactive process between the teacher and student, facilitated by the benefits that technology has to offer.

Unfortunately, there is a lot of additional terminology that inevitably goes with technology and education, and a recent term being used by some people is 'blended learning'. This refers to the use of e-learning 'blended' with face-to-face teaching. However, very few e-learning courses are actually taught with no face-to-face contact at all. Even ODL courses expect the students to meet face-to-face for brief residential sessions during the year. Therefore, so-called blended learning is just another take on e-learning which is already integrated into the face-to-face teaching curriculum.

As mentioned in Chapter 8 (on virtual learning environments), technology provides the platform, i.e. the tools, to deliver teaching and learning activities, but e-learning provides the good practice. As technology developed back in the 1980s and early to mid-1990s, it usually took real enthusiasts to take time out to learn how to use the technology before they could even consider developing teaching resources. Indeed, many staff even took sabbaticals just to learn these new skills. Technology has now evolved to a level that tools such as VLEs mean that teachers need little more than basic word processing skills to deliver resources. It is through this 'empowerment' that e-learning has become a mainstay in education today, and will continue to be so.

A cautionary note about e-learning

When the Web caught on and teachers realised that they could easily transfer their notes online, many thought this was the answer to all their teaching problems. Students could access the notes at any time or place they wanted and staff could cut down on the amount of teaching because the students already had the material. Students would somehow understand the material more easily and be able to pass their exams. This is where many people's approach to e-learning falls down, because they see e-learning simply as a replacement for face-to-face teaching.

E-learning will only add value to the learning process if both staff and students alike approach it with a clear view of what is to be achieved. From the staff point of view, e-learning must be embedded within the curriculum, with well thought out delivery mechanisms and learning outcomes that provide appropriate support for students. From the students' point of view, they must appreciate that, with the greater flexibility afforded them in the manner, time and format with which they can access resources, comes responsibility. Students can no longer expect to be spoon-fed if e-learning provides all the means and resources to allow them to take control of their own learning.

THE BENEFITS OF E-LEARNING

Despite the many years of research undertaken in the area of e-learning, there is still conflicting evidence about whether or not e-learning actually improves the learning process. For example, Neil Selwyn (1999) argues that online learning does not necessarily offer better ways of learning, but provides a different context in which traditional learning can take place. Phil Chambers (1999) suggests that multimedia technology can promote and enhance a range of skills associated with deep level learning. Both arguments are valid and represent fairly common attitudes that e-learning simply provides traditional learning, although in a different environment, or that it can actually *improve* learning.

Following on from this, it could be argued that if e-learning is comparable with face-to-face teaching, then e-learning can be a viable alternative to traditional teaching and learning. This issue is still hotly contested. Either way, one can argue that there are real educational benefits to be gained from e-learning if the result is at least comparable with certain face-to-face teaching and learning activities.

Another argument is that traditional teaching and learning is unlikely to be improved by e-learning as the real benefits come from the interaction between teacher and student. This comes about from the delivery of content and feedback between student and teacher to ascertain levels of understanding. If the student has not understood the content, they can ask questions and be given further help by the teacher. As long as the same principles of feedback and support are provided within an online environment, e-learning can provide an important complementary role to face-to-face teaching.

In addition to all the pedagogical benefits, there are a number of practical benefits where e-learning can help with teaching and learning. e-learning can provide:

- savings in time and money;
- wider access to limited resources;
- better access for students (widening participation);
- faster delivery of assessment;
- improved communication links.

ENGAGING WITH E-LEARNING

Have a purpose in mind

Sometimes people attempt to use e-learning for the wrong reasons; that is, they may simply try to use the technology because it exists or because their colleagues use it, without really understanding how they themselves can benefit from engaging with e-learning. Therefore, the first step to planning for the use of e-learning is to have a goal in mind.

Consider some of the challenges facing teaching and learning, as highlighted in Chapter 8 on VLEs:

- increased student numbers;
- increasing assessment marking;
- widening participation;
- limited teaching resources.

Engaging in e-learning can help tackle these challenges. In addition, the adoption of e-learning can also provide variety to traditional teaching and learning methods in a way that helps support students and maintain interest.

By being aware of the various tools a VLE has to offer (as detailed in Chapter 8), it is possible to select a purpose for using e-learning. There are wide-ranging possibilities, but some of the common benefits include:

- improved communication methods;
- automated assessment;
- interactive content delivery.

Once you have decided upon a purpose for using e-learning, it is possible to plan your work with a clear understanding of what you hope to achieve.

Plan the work

As with any approach to teaching and learning, all activities must be planned and any resources or content must be prepared and checked before they are given to the students. The following quick checklist of questions provides a format for planning this work:

- Have I thought about how the quality/efficiency of my teaching may be supported by the use of e-learning?
- Have I thought about how I want to use e-learning to support teaching and learning?
- Have I allowed enough time to prepare my resources and put them online in time for my planned teaching commitments?

The template below (Figure 9.1) is an example of a form which can be used as a way of outlining e-learning proposals. You may use this type of form to provide an overview of how you intend to use e-learning to support teaching and learning.

PRODUCE AN EVALUATION OUTLINE

An important part of engaging with e-learning is evaluating the outcomes, which should be planned alongside the development of the e-learning resources. This ensures that the overall purpose(s) for using e-learning can be evaluated effectively by setting in place methods of evaluation which will provide the relevant data. As with any evaluation, if the feedback appears negative, for example, 'the students didn't

E-learning initiative		
Primary contact name		Department
Tel. no.		
Email address		
Other staff members involved		

Module title	
No. of students (approx.)	
Start date	
End date (e.g. end of term)	

Rationale for using e-learning

Purpose of use (tick all that apply)

☐	Communication	☐	Content delivery
☐	Assessment	☐	Distribute PowerPoint presentations
☐	Problem solving	☐	Online student collaboration
☐	Online feedback		
☐	Other (please specify below)		

FIGURE 9.1 E-learning pro forma for using a VLE

E-learning initiative – evaluation	
Primary contact name Tel no. Email address	Department
Module title Number of students	
Start date	
Rationale for using e-learning	
Expected outcomes	
Method of evaluation	
Type of data collected	
Student feedback	
Evaluation summary	
Proposals for future development	

FIGURE 9.2 Sample pro forma for planning evaluation

like . . .', this does not automatically mean failure. All evaluation is positive as it provides insights into what may have worked well and, in the light of things that didn't work well, it provides valuable feedback on how to develop things in future. Figure 9.2 shows a sample pro forma which can be used to outline the evaluation method and summary of results.

Depending on how e-learning is used to support teaching and learning, for example, to encourage communication or for interactive content delivery, you may decide to use a student questionnaire to gain feedback. Any such questionnaire has to be planned at the start so that relevant questions are designed to elicit the relevant data which can be used to assess the effectiveness of e-learning in the given context, i.e. if the aim is to focus on the use of communication tools, then the questions should ask about the communication tools.

Although questionnaires are a common way of obtaining feedback, it is also possible to evaluate e-learning by collecting other data. If, say, student support was becoming progressively time-consuming due to increased student numbers, data could be collected on how much staff time was spent with the support of e-learning. To achieve this, a diary could be kept of staff time dedicated to student support. This is an example where the evaluation has to be planned before the work commences and not as an afterthought.

SUMMARY CHECKLIST FOR USING E-LEARNING

- Have a clear purpose for adopting e-learning;
- prepare appropriate evaluation methods;
- plan your work;
- allow plenty of time for the development of resources and implementation;
- evaluate the outcomes;
- implement developments based on feedback.

E-LEARNING IN THE DISCIPLINES

Supporting seminars for English students

Seminars provide students with the opportunity to explore their under-standing of a subject by discussing content with their peers and the teacher. The teacher is able to guide student discussions and help clarify points that students have not fully understood or provide feedback to affirm student conceptions about key topics.

Although a seminar is an ideal opportunity to review work and explore ideas, students sometimes do not do the preparatory reading or don't understand what is expected of them. The result is that the seminar can sometimes turn into a mini-lecture where the teacher is the only person in a position to discuss the content. Another potential problem with the seminar is the limited teaching time allocated to students each week. The following example is based on work by an English lecturer, Lesley Coote, who faced such problems in her English seminars.

FIGURE 9.3 Screenshot of Chaucer module

A VLE is used to provide all the background information to the seminar series, such as module outline, topics to be discussed during each seminar and preparatory questions. A screenshot of the content within the VLE is shown in Figure 9.3. The module is based around Chaucer's *Canterbury Tales* and the history of the period. The students are expected to chair the seminars in pairs, which provides them with the incentive to undertake the preparatory work.

Each week, students are given background information and links to resources based on the forthcoming topic. Additional resources such as images or photographs are provided, together with preparatory questions. Any content used is copyright cleared, for example, photographs which are owned by the lecturer.

During the seminar the students discuss the issues raised on the VLE in the weeks prior to the class. Notes and summaries of the seminar are posted on the VLE after the session. The summaries are deliberately restricted in length and content so that students still only gain the full benefit by attending the seminar. Since face-to-face contact is restricted to the actual seminar due to timetable constraints, discussion boards are also used by the students to discuss issues online. This overcomes the problems of tutor support outside the actual seminar and avoids future classes turning into question-and-answer sessions, allowing more time for in-depth discussion.

The benefits of e-learning in this example highlight how students are able to access resources to prepare for face-to-face teaching and learning. Improved communication is possible by overcoming timetable constraints and the seminar summaries become revision aids, acting as additional resources. E-learning supports the face-to-face teaching by enabling more in-depth and informed discussions to take place, avoiding the problem of a non-interactive, tutor-led seminar.

Computer-assisted assessment (CAA) in biological sciences

With ever-increasing student numbers, assessment takes up more and more time to administer and mark. CAA can help reduce the burden of assessment by automating the process, particularly early on in a course when core classes tend to have larger numbers of students enrolled. This example is based on one teacher's need to assess level one biology students, where numbers had expanded to over 110 and marking a formal test was becoming increasingly time-consuming.

Previously, students were given a paper-based multiple-choice test to assess some core concepts and knowledge about a microbiology module. This was level one content, so the multiple-choice test was deemed appropriate for the purpose. Students were given one hour to complete the test. Each test paper then had to be manually marked and the results entered into a spreadsheet which could be entered into the student records system. Each paper took an estimated 5 minutes to mark, totalling over 9 hours' work. These marks then had to be manually entered into the spreadsheet, taking a further hour or so.

In order to improve this process, CAA was adopted to reduce the demand on staff time and was delivered via a VLE. The computer room used for the test only held 30 computers, so the students were divided into 4 groups and took the test in turn. Figures 9.4 and 9.5 show examples of the questions given. This means that the original one-hour test now takes four hours to administer. However, once all the students have taken the test, there is very little further time involved on the teacher's behalf.

The VLE automatically marks the student tests and produces the results which can be imported directly into a spreadsheet. This process only

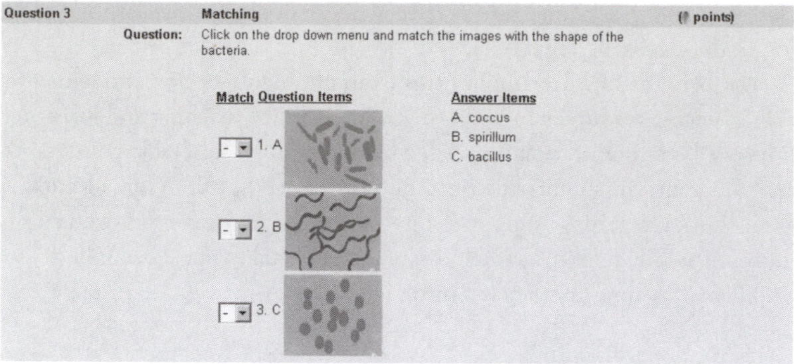

FIGURE 9.4 Matching order question type for identifying microorganisms

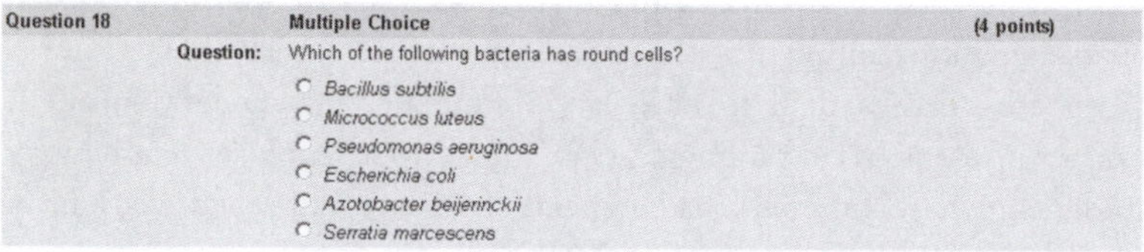

FIGURE 9.5 Standard multiple-choice question type

takes a minute or so to undertake. The time savings for adopting CAA are obvious, but there are also other advantages. The fact that marking is done automatically ensures that there is no potential for human error when marking the tests or when entering marks into the spreadsheet.

The assessment tool also allows various forms of feedback, ranging from just a mark, to detailed comments about each answer. The result is that students gain timely feedback on their performance, which would otherwise be delayed on the paper-based test. This makes CAA beneficial for both summative and formative assessment.

From the teacher's point of view, automated electronic analysis allows confidence testing to be carried out on the questions. This is a way of checking how appropriate certain questions are. For example, is a particular question too easy or too hard? This can help teachers when reviewing their lecture notes, perhaps reviewing particular topics in more depth if the students appear to have difficulty understanding anything.

Promoting group activities in politics

The benefits of group collaboration are well documented and include aspects such as: peer support, sharing of ideas, a sense of ownership with the work and development of transferable skills. There are also benefits for teachers too, including: promoting new approaches to teaching and learning; time management gains from dealing with groups rather than individual students; and the ability to lead discussions which are topical and fresh.

One example of this work is for a politics module with the support of e-learning to foster group-based activities online. With about 65 full- and part-time students on the module, students are split into groups of 6–8 and engage in group activities based on exploring a 'global issue' which is chosen by the students. Issues include global warming, child labour, money laundering etc.

Each group explores the nature of a global issue through a series of set tasks (including building up their own 'virtual library' of resources). The outcomes of each task are evaluated and lead to a re-examination of the issue under investigation. Groups present findings to the class at the end of the course. Activities include exploring political issues and mimicking elections by using VLE tools to get students to 'vote' online. The outcomes are published and used as primers for further discussions.

By adopting e-learning for this approach to teaching and learning, there is a wide range of advantages, such as the benefits of general group work already mentioned. In addition to this, since students can access the resources and activities outside of the classroom, barriers to time and space are circumvented. The activities help support, engage and motivate learners, and since the interactive nature of the work is radically different from traditional teaching, there is increased enthusiasm for the subject.

Due to the plethora of wide-ranging electronic services, such as those provided by news corporations, government organisations and other institutions, it is possible to provide students with links to all these resources. Students are quickly able to find information and news in ways previously denied through traditional media or, at best, at a much slower rate. This means that content for the module is relevant and up-to-date. All the available resources, activities and support ensure that the learning experience provided by e-learning complements the face-to-face teaching and learning.

📖 FURTHER READING

Brown, Sally and Smith, Brenda (1997) *Getting to Grips with Assessment*, Birmingham: Staff and Educational Development Association Publications.

Brown, Sally, Bull, Joanna and Race, Phil (1999) *Computer-assisted Assessment in Higher Education*, London: Kogan Page.

e-Learning Centre, available online at http://www.e-learningcentre.co.uk/eclipse/index.html (accessed 04/08/03).

Salmon, Gilly (2002) *E-tivities: The Key to Active Online Learning*, London: Kogan Page.

Chapter 10

Field trips

The term 'field trip' generally refers to a location-based or field-based visit where students are able to immerse themselves in the scenery and atmosphere of their surroundings. Students are able to engage in a variety of learning activities such as experiencing locations, cultures or even architectural structures first-hand. They are also able to make observations, record data and take samples to reinforce their understanding of the subject being taught.

Since the term 'field' suggests physically being in a field, the inference is often used to define as field trip an excursion for geography students. Although field trips are integral to many geography courses, they are by no means exclusive and field trips can cover a range of subject disciplines.

The subject of geography covers a multitude of subdisciplines, ranging from physical geography/geology to human geography. Therefore, a field trip to a physical geographer may involve an archetypal visit to a place of geographical interest, but a human geography field trip may involve a visit to a village or city. Extending this to other subjects, language students may visit a city for linguistic and cultural purposes, and art or science students may visit a museum or other location of relevant significance. Therefore, the use of a field trip to support teaching and learning offers advantages that span a whole range of subjects.

ADVANTAGES OF FIELD TRIPS

Since field trips, by their very nature, are based on practical skills, e.g. they often involve activities, they share a lot of similar advantages with those gained through laboratory work, including the development of:

Dr Bell was always immersed in field work

- practical skills in the use of specialised equipment and specific techniques;
- observation, measurement and data-recording skills;
- written and oral presentation skills;
- good team-working skills;
- enthusiasm and interest in the subject;
- the ability to apply theory to practice, thus putting the subject into context.

In addition, field trips also offer additional benefits due to the fact that students are out on location and often include residential visits. These benefits include:

- testing and sampling things on a larger scale;
- putting subject into context in relation to the real world;
- the development of self-confidence;
- a good social experience.

A cautionary note about field trips

Although there are great benefits to be had from taking students on field trips, there are also some potential disadvantages and problems associated with them. A fundamental issue is the cost associated with travel and accommodation. Many institutions often subsidise the cost of field trips, but students still have to pay some costs, usually several hundred pounds. This can cause problems if students cannot afford to pay, since they are potentially being denied a comparable learning experience with their peers who can afford to pay.

In addition, there are occasionally health and safety issues where the institution has to ensure that all necessary precautions are taken to avoid risks to the students. Apart from physical safety, there are also medical issues to consider, for example, students who may have special medical needs (diabetics, epileptics etc.) or special dietary requirements (such as for lactose intolerants). Gender and cultural issues can also cause problems with field trips. Some females are reluctant to visit places if they particularly feel at risk or if there is an issue of sharing accommodation, which could also concern people with religious viewpoints.

There are also a number of logistical issues to consider when undertaking a field trip. If a remote location is being visited, travel arrangements may be difficult. Additional concerns include: the risk of damaging the environment if the site is of particular ecological significance; cultural problems of offending local populations; or simple logistical problems such as language barriers.

A very important issue, especially with the 2002 SENDA legislation, is the need to take into account the needs of disabled students when considering a field trip. There are issues such as providing an amanuensis (someone to take notes and copy work) for a partially sighted student or providing access for students with other forms of disability. However, there are wider issues concerning disability and accessibility.

ACCESSIBILITY

When people think about disability and access to field trips, they often think about students in wheelchairs. However, wheelchair-bound people only actually account for about 4 per cent of the total number of disabled people and this figure is smaller for students in education, running at about 2.5 per cent (figure obtained for 2001/2 from the Higher Education Statistics Agency (HESA)). Therefore, careful thought must be given to the planning of field trips to take into account the needs of disabled students.

When thinking about the learning experience afforded by field trips, it is important to define the learning outcomes that you expect students to gain from such a trip. Being clear about your reasons for providing a field trip can help define whether a disabled student actually needs to go on the trip. Are there alternative ways of providing the same learning experience, for example?

Certain field trips may require students visiting inaccessible places that would involve travelling over difficult terrain or climbing. This may restrict access to wheelchair-bound students, but it could also affect partially sighted students or even students who suffer from vertigo. Although there is no real substitute for a field trip, i.e. actually visiting a location, by considering the learning outcomes it is possible to offer learning experiences that are similar, or at least cover most of the benefits of a field trip. Many of these alternatives can be offered through the use of technology.

VIRTUAL FIELD TRIPS

Virtual field trips have been developed over the years using computer technology to give students the experience of visiting a location without

Dr Bell takes his students on a tour of Mount Everest with the 'Virtua 3000' virtual reality headsets

actually being there. They usually come in two basic formats. The more common type available tend to be interactive 'visits' created for a website, where students can link to information and images. The second type concerns actual 'virtual reality' technology which allows three-dimensional or panoramic views of a location, giving students 360° views and enabling them to zoom in and out for closer or wider inspections.

The idea of a virtual field trip has evolved partly to avoid some of the potential problems of actual field trips, but also to offer access to additional field trips which students might otherwise never visit or experience. Another important reason for the development of virtual field trips is that they can act as a valuable precursor to field trips. The only potential disadvantage of virtual field trips is the time taken to develop them, but offset against the longer-term time and cost savings this could actually be considered a valid reason for their development.

WHAT ARE THE BENEFITS?

Both teachers and students can benefit from the use of virtual field trips. The benefits to students include:

- greater student autonomy in using resources;
- observation of the location through well-prepared images and photographs;
- the ability to undertake random and repeated sample or data collections;
- quick access to data analysis software and other utilities for timely results;
- access to a range of online information resources for additional help and support;
- comparison of a range of virtual field trips;
- the ability to practise skills and techniques required for actual field trips;
- high interest for students.

As well as the benefits of virtual field trips for students, there are also a number of benefits for teachers:

- students are guaranteed to see the information and images you want them to see;

- observations and data recordings are not dependent on circumstances outside your control, such as adverse weather conditions;
- extra background information, images or photographs, help and exercises can be provided;
- familiarisation with the location can better prepare students for the actual field trip;
- the value of the actual field trip is increased because the students will have prepared for the core activities beforehand;
- there is the opportunity for students to record more observations and obtain better quality data (because they are better prepared).

WHAT FEATURES CAN A VIRTUAL FIELD TRIP OFFER?

At a very basic level, a virtual field trip can offer a series of linked images and photographs with supporting information and questions that explore the students' underlying knowledge. It can also supply students with information about key aspects of the location and provide open-ended questions which the students can follow up with further study. And it can be used to introduce students to new skills such as sampling or research techniques, for example, where and how to look up public documents relevant to any future visit.

At a more advanced level, a virtual field trip can provide more detailed information, links to searchable databases for specific data and highly interactive exercises that mimic the real experiences of a field trip. One such example is a historical virtual field trip to a city, where students can explore various aspects of the location. Photographs give examples of what the city looks like, and access to searchable public or government records provides information about the population and its demographics. In addition, hypertext links (electronic non-sequential links) and interactive 'clickable' images can be used to provide additional information about key terms or structures, such as significant architectural designs.

At a still further level of design are virtual field trips that not only provide the levels of use already discussed, but also tailor the experience to the students' needs. One example of this is the ability to take virtual samples or make data recordings based on options chosen by the student. To mimic the experience of doing this for real, algorithms (mathematical ways of randomising output) can be built in to provide different results. Students then have to analyse this data and evaluate their significance. The overall result is a virtual field trip that exposes students to much of what they would expect in a real field trip, but with a host of other information, support and independence of study.

EXAMPLES FROM THE DISCIPLINES

A virtual field trip around Tenerife for geography students

Richard Middleton at the University of Hull has developed an interactive virtual field trip around Tenerife. This is aimed at preparatory work for students who visit the island as part of an undergraduate level two geography course. The virtual field trip is tied in with laboratory exercises and post-visit activities in the form of workshops to discuss student projects that form part of the assessment.

The laboratory exercises include the opportunity for students to view and work with rock samples common to Tenerife to prepare them for the real experience. Students also develop skills in using GPS (Global Positioning System) equipment, which uses satellite technology to locate your position with an accuracy of a few metres. The students also have a practical session to develop group working skills to prepare them for their time together at Tenerife. Another important activity is the use of the field notebook, which is an important skill required for recording observations and data. All these activities, including the use of the virtual field trip, are compulsory.

When the students actually visit Tenerife, they take laptops with them to use for a range of purposes. One of the activities the students undertake while they are on the field trip is to prepare and deliver PowerPoint presentations. This helps students to practise giving presentations using technology, an approach endorsed by Pauline Kneale, a national teaching fellow at Leeds University, who promotes the use of student presentations within her own teaching.

Due to the way the virtual field trip is tied in with the laboratory activities, there are a number of benefits that help prepare the students for the actual field trip. The students are introduced to new skills which they will use while they are in Tenerife, including sampling rocks and recording appropriate observations and data in their field notebooks. The virtual field trip enables students to review information about the island according to their needs and quickly access other information via the Web. One relevant point Richard Middleton commented on was to say: 'Using the Web is often more natural to students than reading a book.'

In terms of accessibility, this field trip holds no greater barriers for disabled students than any other field trip situation. In fact, the field trip has previously taken a partially sighted student with an amanuensis and experienced no problems. The added benefit of the pre- and post-field trip activities, coupled with the virtual field trip, actually has the potential to provide much of the skills and experience for any disabled student who may not be able to travel.

A virtual field trip around Paris for humanities students

There is a wide range of virtual field trips now available on the Web, also commonly referred to as virtual tours. Used in an educational context, these virtual tours of cities can be used for a number of subjects, including language studies or arts subjects. One example is a virtual tour of Paris.

There are different types of Web tours available for Paris, consisting of both 'interactive' sites and full 'virtual reality' sites. Humanities students can use these virtual field trips to view Paris and all its main attractions, including its famous museums. The Louvre is perhaps Paris's most famous art museum, housing Leonardo de Vinci's *Mona Lisa*. The museum offers a virtual reality tour of the Louvre that provides 360° views of the museum and its artefacts.

These tours can be used in a variety of ways, depending on your teaching and learning objectives for your students. Language students can study aspects of city life, including the culture, use of language in different public settings and general language comprehension. Students on arts courses can take virtual tours of museums and obtain in-depth information about different exhibitions. As with the Tenerife virtual field trip, students can undertake various exercises before visiting Paris to prepare them for the activities while there.

If a field trip is planned for a visit to Paris and some of its attractions, a virtual tour website can be used to familiarise the students with each location and to provide additional background information. Alternatively, if a specific museum is the focus of the trip, the students can find out about what artefacts are on show and how to find their way around the museum. In both situations, it is a good idea to prepare an itinerary for the visit so that the most efficient use of time is planned for travelling between attractions.

📖 FURTHER READING

Interactions, the electronic journal of the Educational Technology Service at the University of Warwick, available online at http://www.warwick.ac.uk/ETS/interactions/info.htm (accessed 04/08/03).

Hurst, Stephen (1998) 'Use of "Virtual" Field Trips in Teaching Introductory Geology', *Computers & Geosciences*, 24 (7), pp. 653–8.

Kneale, Pauline, http://www.geog.leeds.ac.uk/people/p.kneale (accessed 07/01/04).

Chapter 11

Laboratory classes

Although the term 'laboratory' often conjures up images of scientists in white coats feverishly working away mixing chemicals in test tubes, there are broader applications in education. In language and linguistics, for example, students are often exposed to laboratory classes that involve the use of audio-visual equipment. Psychology also involves laboratory work of various kinds, such as the study of human responses to various stimuli. Another subject discipline that uses laboratories is sports science, where the subjects being studied are often the students themselves, experimenting with exercise equipment to investigate human physiology.

A laboratory is a specially equipped room where students are able to test out ideas by engaging in practical work. Laboratories allow students to apply their knowledge and develop skills that will be of use to them in real-life situations but in a safe environment. Although certain subject disciplines don't always have a practical skills element to them, there are a number of aspects of laboratory work which are equally beneficial across the board. In this context, therefore, laboratory classes refer to the application of skills and knowledge to real situations where students can test different scenarios.

Ever-expanding developments with C&IT and computer technology in general mean that a lot of equipment used in a laboratory setting has the potential to exploit this technology for educational purposes. Students can combine technology in a variety of ways with laboratory work, from the automated operation of equipment to high-speed recording of data and analysis of results.

ADVANTAGES OF LABORATORY WORK

There are a number of advantages to be gained from involving students in laboratory work. Not all the benefits, however, are directly linked to

The students were made well aware of laboratory
safety procedures by Dr Bell

developing practical skills since students are also able to develop subject-based and interpersonal skills. These include:

- improving scientific enquiry through experimentation, project work and problem solving;
- practical skills that develop familiarity with and dexterity in using specialised equipment and specific techniques;
- other practical skills such as observation, measurement and data-recording skills;
- developing communication skills and reporting succinctly in both written and oral form;
- developing an understanding of the need to adopt a professional, safe attitude when in a real working environment;
- developing good team-work skills;
- fostering enthusiasm and interest in the subject;

145

- being able to put the subject in context by applying theory to practice;
- being able to judge the reliability of data;
- being able to design experiments to test hypotheses.

A cautionary note about laboratory work

While the advantages of engaging in laboratory work are numerous, there are also some issues that can constrain its widespread use. On a practical level, there are issues of time, money and space.

Laboratory work by its very nature is time intensive and the curriculum may simply not allow for much practical work. Also, the need to develop properly equipped laboratories also brings with it financial constraints which institutions cannot always afford. Although many institutions have laboratory space to teach students, the ever-increasing numbers over the years now mean that some courses recruit far more students than can physically fit and work safely in a laboratory. Some departments even resort to splitting the students into groups and repeating laboratory classes in the morning and afternoon just to fit them all in. This effectively doubles the time required for one class. However, technology can help work around some, if not all, of these issues.

USING TECHNOLOGY TO SUPPORT LABORATORY WORK

Laboratory simulations

Students undertaking practical work often only get one chance to do a particular experiment. This may be because laboratory space is at a premium or the experiment costs too much to repeat. The result is that a student gets one chance to practise the skill or record results and, if the experiment fails for some reason, then this learning opportunity is lost.

Part of the learning process in these situations is to do something, observe the results, and draw conclusions based upon the outcomes and prior knowledge. This often takes time for reflection before the students can fully grasp the concept being taught. If they can repeat the procedure more than once or even (ideally) repeatedly, this will be of great benefit.

146

Over the years computer simulations have developed to help students simulate experiments which would otherwise be costly in terms of time, space or even on safety grounds. Although there is often no substitution for the real experiment, simulations can help the student address and answer many of the same problems posed in the real experiment. Although the use of laboratory simulations may seem to contradict the reason for doing actual laboratory work, computer-based simulations can be a useful precursor to real experimentation and also act as a good revision aid. If students are better prepared for a laboratory class after practising with a simulated copy, they are more likely to appreciate and benefit from the actual practical work. They are also more likely to understand the underlying principles and record all relevant data which they might otherwise have been oblivious to.

Data recorders

A major component of laboratory work often involves data gathering. Prior to the advent of digital data recorders, equipment for recording information often involved plotters where a pen produced a graph on a continuous stream of graph paper. This produced copious rolls of paper that had to be analysed manually.

Digital recorders are now able to store data from various sources, including analogue data to record large volumes over extended time periods. This information is converted into a digital format can then be quickly analysed and processed by students using standard software packages such as a spreadsheet. Systems are available such as 'ADI Instruments MacLab' that can record simultaneous channels of data for analysis.

Audio-visual laboratories

The use of audio-video laboratories to support teaching and learning is now commonplace. Many courses, for example, various media studies programmes, have audio and video editing suites which allow students to experiment with specialised equipment to develop specific skills commonly used for industry.

One example is the use of computer software that allows the quick formatting of digitised video and then editing and cutting. This is a more efficient way of working with video as opposed to the original process which left video tape 'on the cutting floor'. Computer technology has advanced so much in recent years that the equipment (digital video cameras) and software are cheaply and readily available in high street shops.

Another common example is the use of computer technology in photography courses. High-quality digital cameras that can 'download' their images straight to the computer are now available. This means that photograph processing is much cheaper and students are able to spend as much time as they like experimenting with processing images. In addition, sophisticated graphic design software allows images to be transformed in a number of ways and students can become quite proficient in the art of computerised image editing.

Computer models

As stated initially, laboratories are no longer simply confined to the realms of the so-called traditional sciences involving scientists in white coats. Computers are now used extensively in a range of computer science and engineering courses to undertake 'virtual' experiments.

Computer Aided Design (CAD) is now a common component of many engineering and computer science courses. These highly specialised software packages enable students to experiment with the design of equipment, tools and other complex products without actually building them. The advantage of this, as with any laboratory situation, is that students can experiment in a safe environment without the need for time-consuming construction and costly materials.

Although this is only ever theoretical work, students are able to test the theories behind products such as stress loads on materials or the durability of resistors in electronic systems. In this way, when they come to design these products for real, they are less likely to make fundamental mistakes. This also reduces the risk of expensive materials being wasted through poor understanding of the subject.

Another advantage of computer models is that they can be used to simulate theoretical systems which are never capable of being tested in real terms. Certain astronomy studies postulate hypotheses resulting from indirect observation and the outcomes can be tested using simulated computer models, based on known information and predictions. In this way, students can experiment with different models to determine outcomes based on known data and observations.

LABORATORY CLASSES IN THE DISCIPLINES

Physical chemistry experiments

At the University of Liverpool, Steve Walker has developed computer experiment simulations to help students studying physical chemistry to understand some basic physics concepts. The tools consist of simulations (and high-quality diagrams and relevant animations) designed to accompany tutorials or workshops. Figure 11.1 shows a screenshot from a simulation of the photoelectric effect illustrating 'threshold energy'.

The simulated experiments are not designed to be used in isolation but are tied closely to the teaching of the theory. As such, the experiments do not impose any formal teaching style and so can be used in a number of ways by the teacher to support the development of understanding of the subject.

The context of this work is that students have access to what may be considered predominantly physics teaching but with a direct application to physical chemistry. This way, students are supported in their

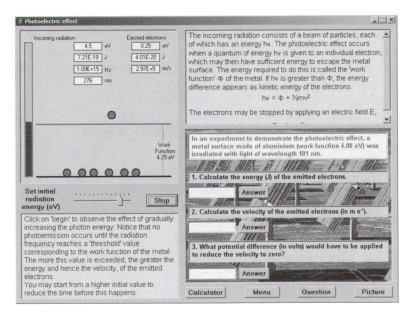

FIGURE 11.1 A simulation of the photoelectric effect illustrating 'threshold energy'

studies through the use of simulated experiments which they can repeat until they fully understand the topic.

Conducting real experiments across the Web

One of the advantages of laboratory equipment becoming increasingly computerised (even toasters and refrigerators are now available equipped with electronic processors) is that the functioning can be increasingly automated. The prospect of automating laboratory work through the Web is now being undertaken by Hugh Cartwright at the University of Oxford, whereby real experiments can be controlled by students operating the equipment via the Web. This means that students and teachers who may not have direct access to specialised or expensive equipment can still run real experiments.

There are a number of advantages to conducting laboratory work in this way, not least because it gives students access to laboratory equipment they may previously have been denied. With access to additional experiments, teachers are able to broaden the range of experiments they can offer students. Students are able to interact with the real experiment and produce real results, rather than simulated data. The duplication of equipment between institutions can also be reduced if laboratory work can be shared in this way. This work is still restricted in its broad applications, but has the potential to be more and more common in the near future.

Collecting and analysing data for sports science experiments

Students doing sports science degrees often undertake laboratory work as part of exercise physiology modules. Digital data recorders can be used to collect data from subjects (usually the students themselves) undergoing various forms of exercise.

Laboratory equipment such as ergometers can be used to examine aerobic power and ventilatory responses to exercise. Students are also able to monitor blood lactate responses to exercise and electrocardiographs under close supervision with the laboratory technician or teacher. This enables students to gain practical experience of laboratory work and familiarise themselves with various testing procedures used in sports science.

FURTHER READING

Boud, David, Dunn, J., Kennedy, T. and Thorley, R. (1980) 'The Aims of Science Laboratory Courses: A Survey of Students, Graduates and Practising Scientists', *European Journal of Science Education*, 2 (4), pp. 415–28 (now called *International Journal of Science Education*).

Cartwright, Hugh (2003) 'Web-based Experiments in Physics and Chemistry', *New Directions in the Teaching of Physical Sciences*, May (published by the LTSN Physical Sciences Centre, Hull).

Labwork in Science Education, available online at http://www.education.leeds.ac.uk/research/scienceed/labwork.htm (accessed 04/08/03).

Chapter 12

Evaluating teaching resources

Although the process and purpose of evaluation may appear obvious, it often isn't considered appropriately by many teachers. These teachers may have taught the same way for years and student pass rates may have been relatively consistent each year. However, as students get older and more mature, they are able to take more control over their own learning. Therefore, the question may be 'Are they learning because of the teacher or despite the teacher?'.

This chapter is not intended to give detailed information about evaluation methods and procedures, but is aimed more at raising the main issues about evaluation. Thus, when you consider the evaluation of technology, you will be more aware of the reasons for evaluating it and be in a better position to evaluate the appropriate components.

Culture is changing in tertiary education. There are moves by the government to professionalise and accredit teaching in higher education, which will mean that teaching at all levels will be formally accredited. In addition, students are also expecting a better quality education because of the increasing fees they must pay. Teaching is therefore becoming more accountable and evaluation plays a pivotal role in improving the quality of teaching and learning.

One of the biggest problems with undertaking effective evaluation is that it is often considered after the event. Therefore, the opportunity to collect the necessary data and information about the effectiveness (or otherwise) of the teaching can be missed. Another big problem when using C&IT to support teaching and learning, especially when piloting new approaches, is that the technology is often blamed if things go wrong or if the students don't like using the technology. However, few people actually consider the possibility that poor content or poor organisation may be at fault rather than the technology alone.

WHAT IS EVALUATION?

Evaluation is the process of verifying that what we do is worthwhile. The process of evaluation in relation to teaching and learning has a number of benefits. Many people assume that evaluation is simply a process for highlighting problems and while this may be partly true, it is not the only purpose of evaluation. If something isn't working as well as we might hope, then proper evaluation can detect this and offer practical solutions. However, a big benefit of evaluation is that it can confirm if things are working, otherwise how will you really know how effective your teaching is?

ISSUES RELATING TO EVALUATION

- Why evaluate?
- What can be achieved by the process?
- What should be assessed?
- What methods can be used?
- Whose viewpoints should be sought?
- How will we act on the data received?

WHY EVALUATE?

There are several reasons why you should evaluate your teaching:

- to assess the quality of your teaching;
- to assess learning outcomes;
- to gauge student attitudes;
- for external quality enhancement (reviews by funding bodies).

Although the first point should be paramount, some teachers never really address this question, perhaps not daring to ask themselves if they are good teachers and never look for ways to develop themselves. The paradox, however, is that these same teachers often submit research papers to external scrutiny and will edit and change things based on peer feedback. It follows, therefore, that teachers should not be afraid of putting their teaching to the same review process.

What can be achieved?   Evaluation can improve the individual's teaching skills and the quality of the teaching materials. It can also help improve the wider teaching process.

153

What should be assessed? This question partly depends on what the individual wishes to review. As a teacher, you may wish to assess your teaching style, for example, or assess the quality of your handouts and how the students use them. A more difficult consideration is trying to measure the 'success' of your teaching: should student marks be taken as a measure, for example?

What methods can be used? There are a number of evaluation methods available but not all will necessarily be suitable, or possible, depending on the circumstances. Methods of evaluation include observation, interviews, questionnaires, measuring outcomes (e.g. exam results or general quality of student work).

Whose viewpoints should be sought? There are several sources of information that can be used for evaluation. The obvious sources are the students themselves, but colleagues can also provide useful viewpoints or even other sources such as external examiners or independent reviewers.

How will you act on the data received? Evaluation is pointless if nothing is done with the data. So will you ignore it, argue against it, accept it wholeheartedly or accept it with reservations?

THE EVALUATION CYCLE

Evaluation is not a finite process, but an ongoing cycle of review and adaptation. Even if your teaching is effective and student satisfaction is high, the content may need updating to ensure that the students are informed about the latest research in your subject discipline. Figure 12.1 shows a simple evaluation cycle which must be addressed continually so that the teaching and learning process does not stagnate.

When considering the evaluation cycle, there are several questions you must ask yourself:

- Do I need to change anything?
- What evidence do I have that I do/don't need to change anything?
- How do I check that any changes made are effective?
- Do I need to change anything?

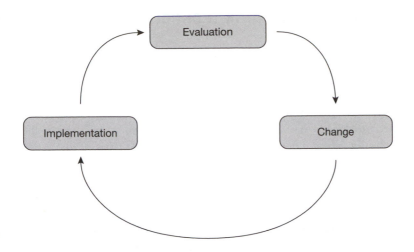

■ **FIGURE 12.1** Evaluation cycle

CIRO APPROACH TO EVALUATION

There are a number of approaches that you can adopt when considering the process of evaluation, of which the CIRO approach is one example:

Context evaluation
Input evaluation
Reaction evaluation
Outcomes evaluation

Context – What needs to be changed?   Find out what needs to be changed and decide how to change it.

Input – What procedures are most likely to bring about changes?
Ascertain what methods can be used.

Reaction – Obtaining student reactions
Obtain feedback from students to gain their reactions.

Outcome – What evidence is there that change has occurred?
Determine whether changes have been effective and use this information to improve subsequent teaching.

155 ■

THE BENEFITS OF USING TECHNOLOGY FOR EVALUATION

Evaluation is based around gathering information and data related to what you are evaluating, in this case teaching and learning. The evaluation of teaching is often based on student questionnaires that are paper-based. Administering paper questionnaires is time-consuming and can create storage headaches, especially if a department has to store the results for many different modules or courses. Analysis of the questionnaire is also time-consuming as it will take staff a significant amount of time to analyse the feedback.

The use of technology can help avoid these problems as evaluation can be administered electronically (for example, delivering computerised questionnaires) and the results can be quickly analysed. An additional benefit of using technology is that data can be stored efficiently and can be retrieved at short notice. This also means that different sets of evaluation data can be easily compared with each other, for example, by comparing data from different years based on changes to the curriculum.

EVALUATING THE TECHNOLOGY

There are two aspects to evaluation and the use of computer technology. The first is evaluating the effectiveness of the technology in the support of teaching and learning; the second is the use of technology as a method for evaluation. There are a number of options when using technology to evaluate and these will be covered in the next section.

When using C&IT to support teaching and learning, it is easy to blame, or indeed praise, the technology when it comes to evaluation. However, it is important that the outcomes are assessed appropriately to identify clearly what effects C&IT has on the learning process. For example, if technology is adopted within a course or module and the student response is favourable, is this because the technology has enhanced the learning process or is it simply because a different approach, i.e. using technology, made the subject more interesting?

One example of research that demonstrates this point is work done by Roy Rada (1998) who evaluated the effectiveness of three different 'groupware' systems for supporting student learning. (Groupware is a generic term for software that enables group interactions, such as discussion boards and file sharing.) With the first system, student satisfaction with the learning process was high, but the teacher found the use of technology time-consuming, taking longer, in fact, than offering formal lectures. The second system proved less popular with the students. But the third system was approved by the students and proved less time-intensive for the teacher.

This work suggests that the technology alone does not have a direct effect on the quality of the learning process, but it is how the technology is combined with the teaching method that can affect outcomes. Therefore, in terms of evaluation, it is important to identify the factors that contribute to the effectiveness of the learning experience. In this case, the level of online teacher interaction with students was a key factor in improving the learning process when *coupled* with technology – and this is a very important distinction to make.

It can be difficult to evaluate the value of incorporating technology into teaching if the reasons for using it in the first place aren't clear. In the example just given, was the motivation for using technology to improve the learning process or to save teaching contact time? If you are clear right from the start about what you want to achieve, it will be easier to evaluate the technology. This is why, as stated already, it is important to plan your evaluation before you actually undertake any work.

C&IT METHODS TO EVALUATE TEACHING AND LEARNING

Depending on the reason for using technology to support teaching and learning, it is possible to use the technology itself to evaluate the benefits, or technology can simply be used to evaluate traditional face-to-face teaching. The following methods highlight some of the main ways in which technology can be used for evaluation.

Questionnaires

The use of questionnaires is probably the most common method available for evaluating teaching. In many instances students are given a paper-based questionnaire evaluation form to complete and the teacher then collates the data manually and analyses the results. This approach is fine with small numbers of students, but for large classes the questionnaire can be time-consuming to administer and process.

The use of electronic questionnaires can greatly reduce the time taken to administer an evaluation form and can also allow automatic analysis of the results. Students simply complete the evaluation forms online and teachers can access the data from their own computer. There are a number of products available which enable you to produce and administer questionnaires without the need for advanced C&IT skills.

Many virtual learning environments now have survey tools built in which can deliver questionnaires, or separate assessment products which also offer anonymous surveys. Students can complete the questionnaire at a computer in their own time, which removes any criticism of bias or influence when students are asked to complete the questionnaire in class when the teacher is present.

Although there is the ongoing problem of encouraging students to complete the questionnaire, this argument equally applies to paper questionnaires. To encourage greater response, students can be given incentives to complete their forms. In some examples, students have been offered book tokens, though this can prove costly for continual evaluation, so other incentives such as providing further resources or student marks upon completion often encourages a greater response.

Confidence testing

If computer-assisted assessment is used as part of a module or course, the results can be used as an evaluation indicator. It is possible to undertake what is called 'confidence testing' of the assessment to evaluate how appropriate each question is in relation to what is being assessed. For example, if confidence testing shows that students are performing poorly on a particular topic based on the questions being asked, then this can be used to inform the teaching process. That is, the teacher could consider spending more time in a lecture focusing on that topic in order to help students gain a better understanding. Conversely, if students consistently score high marks on something, this is an indicator that they already know this topic or that it is taught particularly well.

User statistics

When students use C&IT as part of a course or module, it is possible to monitor the levels of use or access. This information can tell us a great deal about student use of technology. If students have difficulty understanding a topic even though additional resources are available online, a review of access levels can show how often students are accessing the material.

This information can show whether the students are simply not using the support material and, if not, further investigation can explore the problem. It may be that there are barriers to access or the students have been given insufficient motivation; or the technology itself may be a barrier to accessing resources. If statistics show that students are accessing the material, then further evaluation may explore the quality and clarity of the resources provided. Therefore, using access statistics can be a very valuable evaluation tool to determine the effectiveness of technology and the resources provided by it.

Exam results

Using exam results can be a very dubious approach to evaluating the effectiveness of teaching and learning for a number of reasons. However, exams are the core method of evaluating the learning process; if students pass, the teaching can be deemed to be effective. There has been a lot of research into the effectiveness of teaching and some people argue that true learning cannot be evaluated through the immediacy of exams. Indeed, it has been suggested that the full benefits of learning may not even become apparent for up to two years later.

Taking a more pragmatic approach to evaluating the learning process through exams, one could argue that if the teaching is effective, i.e. students understand the subject thoroughly, then they will inevitably perform better under examination. An example of this is teachers who have developed multimedia resources on CD for their own students. The students have been using the CD for three years and analysis of the associated exam results show that average exam results increased in the first two years but dipped slightly in year three, though each year showed a good pass rate.

Since only three years' results are available, it is impossible to identify a trend, or explain if results from year three were simply down to statistical fluctuation. The caveat here and with exams in general, is that there are other factors involved, for example, social factors, so the exam marks themselves cannot be relied on too heavily.

EVALUATION IN THE DISCIPLINES

Student questionnaire for history students

History students use a virtual learning environment as part of a level one module. Since one of the learning outcomes is to develop skills in using the Web and general Windows software, the use of a VLE provides a means for demonstrating these skills. In addition, since the VLE used offers a tool to deliver anonymous questionnaires, the end-of-module evaluation was carried out online. Figure 12.2 shows a screenshot of part of the evaluation questionnaire.

The students are given the questionnaire to complete in their own time and the VLE automatically analyses the results. All questions are anonymous, so students cannot be identified by their responses. There is a range of question types available, including multiple choice and text responses. This enables quantitative and qualitative evaluation to be carried out. The teacher is able to analyse the results and act accordingly, based on student feedback.

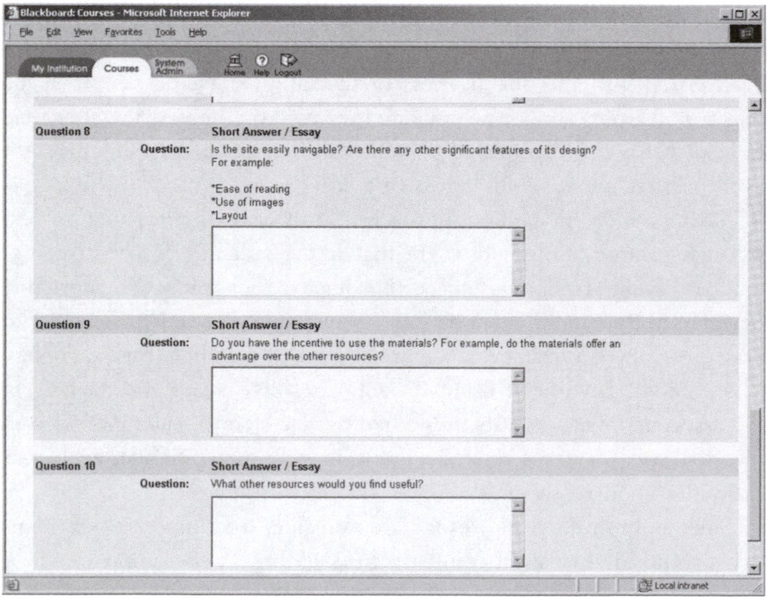

FIGURE 12.2 Screenshot of online student questionnaire

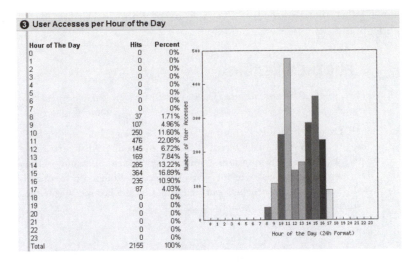

❸ User Accesses per Hour of the Day

Hour of The Day	Hits	Percent
0	0	0%
1	0	0%
2	0	0%
3	0	0%
4	0	0%
5	0	0%
6	0	0%
7	0	0%
8	37	1.71%
9	107	4.96%
10	250	11.60%
11	476	22.08%
12	145	6.72%
13	169	7.84%
14	285	13.22%
15	364	16.89%
16	235	10.90%
17	87	4.03%
18	0	0%
19	0	0%
20	0	0%
21	0	0%
22	0	0%
23	0	0%
Total	2155	100%

FIGURE 12.3 Screenshot of user statistics showing access at times of the day

User statistics on a biology module

Students on a level one biology module are given access to a VLE as a means of providing a range of support materials. Students also use the assessment tool to take several formative assessments during the module. There are about 160 students on the module, so the online assessment saves time on manual marking.

A week prior to each online test the students are given access to a mock test. This helps the students become familiar with the type of test they will be given the following week, including the type of questions that will be asked. Despite this support, several students don't perform as well as the rest of the class. There could be a number of reasons for this, but by checking the statistics it is possible to identify students who are not attempting the mock test. Figure 12.3 shows a screenshot of some statistics that can be accessed from the VLE.

Student motivation is one obvious factor for the successful adoption of C&IT within teaching and learning. Since it is possible to identify students who are not using the technology, further investigation can help find solutions to this problem. Another interesting observation with this module is that the classes (and all assessment) end before the Christmas break. However, checking access over the Christmas period showed that there were over 700 log-ins or 'hits', even though the students had completed the module.

📖 FURTHER READING

Forsyth, Ian, Joliffe, Alan and Stevens, David (1999) *Evaluating a Course: Practical Strategies for Teachers, Lecturers and Trainers*, 2nd edn, London: Kogan Page.

McConnell, David (2001) 'Researching Networked Learning: Issues Arising from the Use of a Variety of Different Research Methods', 9th International Student Learning Symposium, 'Improving Student Learning Using Learning Technologies', Heriot-Watt University, Edinburgh, Scotland, 9–11 September. Proceedings published by Oxford Brookes Centre for Staff and Learning Development.

Bibliography

Adobe GoLive, http://www.adobe.com/products/golive/main.html (accessed 16/06/03)

Alessi, Stephen M. and Trollip, Stanley R. (2001) *Multimedia for Learning*, 3rd edn, Massachusetts: Allyn and Bacon

Anderson, Alistair and Chin, Paul (2000) *Delivering MCQs Via the Web, Innovations in Teaching*, Educational Development Team Publication, Institute for Learning, University of Hull

Athens, http://www.athens.ac.uk/ (accessed 30/06/03)

Boud, David, Dunn, Jeffrey, Hegarty-Hazel, Elizabeth (1989) *Teaching in Laboratories*, Guildford: Open University Press

The British Library, http://www.bl.uk/ (accessed 30/06/03)

British Library Public Catalogue, http://blpc.bl.uk/ (accessed 30/06/03)

BUBL, http://www.bubl.ac.uk/ (accessed 30/06/03)

Cartwright, Hugh (2001) 'Creating a Central Role for Online Experiments in the Undergraduate Science Course', LTSN Physical Sciences Development Project, report available online at http://www.physsci.ltsn.ac.uk/devprojs/online_expts.htm (accessed 06/01/04)

Cascade Multimedia Interactive Training Unit, Institute for Learning, University of Hull, available online at http://www.cascade.hull.ac.uk/index.html (accessed 18/05/03)

Chambers, Phil (1999) 'Information Handling Skills, Cognition and New Technologies', *British Journal of Educational Technology*, 30 (2), pp. 151–62

Chin, Paul (2002) *Virtual Learning Environments*, Briefing Paper, published by LTSN Physical Sciences Centre, Hull, available online at http://www.physsci.ltsn.ac.uk (accessed 30/06/03)

Chin, Paul (2002) *Virtual/Managed Learning Environments*, Toolkit, published by LTSN Physical Sciences Centre, Hull, available online at http://www.physsci.ltsn.ac.uk (accessed 30/06/03)

163

Chin, Paul (2003) *Virtual Learning Environments*, Practice Guide, published by LTSN Physical Sciences Centre, Hull, available online at http//www.physsci.ltsn.ac.uk (accessed 30/06/03)

Chin, Paul and Waugh, David (Educational Development Team) (1999) 'Preparing Teaching Materials', unpublished course notes for Higher Education Teaching Diploma, University of Hull

COPAC, http://copac.ac.uk/ (accessed 30/06/03)

Corel WordPerfect, http://www.corel.com/servlet/Satellite?pagename= Corel/Products/productInfo&id=1042153063297 (accessed 16/06/03)

EBSCO, http://www.ebsco.com (accessed 30/06/03)

'e-Learning: the future of learning', Cirencester: eLearnity, available online at http://www.elearnity.com (accessed 01/07/03)

Ellington, Henry and Race, Phil (1993) *Producing Teaching Materials*, 2nd edn, London: Kogan Page

Endnote, http://www.endnote.com.

European Computer Driving Licence (ECDL), http://www.ecdl.co.uk (accessed 16/06/03)

Fawkes, Steven (1999) *Switched On? Video Resources in Modern Language Settings: Modern Languages in Practice*, Clevedon: Multilingual Matters

Ferl, Information service for all staff working within the post compulsory education sector, http://ferl.becta.org.uk/ (accessed 18/05/03)

'A Framework for Pedagogical Evaluation of Virtual Learning Environments' (1999) JTAP Report 41, now archived at http://www.jisc.ac.uk (accessed 07/02/04)

Google, http://www.google.com/ (accessed 30/06/03)

Grandgenett, Neal, Grandgenett, Don, Topp, Neal, Fluckiger, Jarene *et al.* (1997) 'Integrating Technology into Teaching and Learning: The Three Keys to the Kingdom', *Innovations in Education and Training International*, 34 (4), pp. 252–6

Hill, Brian (1989) *Making the Most of Video*, London: Centre for Information on Language Teaching and Research

Hill, Brian (1999) *Video in Language Learning*, Grantham: Centre for Information on Language Teaching and Research

Historical Abstracts, http://serials.abc-clio.com/ (accessed 30/06/03)

Honey P. and Mumford, A. (1986) *The Manual of Learning Styles,* 2nd edn, Maidenhead: Peter Honey

Joint Information Systems Committee, TechDis service, http://www.techdis.ac.uk/ (accessed 30/06/03)

Joint Information Systems Committee (JISC) http://www.jisc.ac.uk (accessed 30/06/03)

Kolb, David A. (1984) *Experiential Learning*, Englewood Cliffs, NJ: Prentice Hall

Learning and Teaching Support Network (LTSN), http://www.ltsn.ac.uk (accessed 30/06/03)

Louvre Museum, http://www.louvre.or.jp/ (accessed 29/05/03)

Macromedia Dreamweaver, http://www.macromedia.com/software/dreamweaver/ (accessed 16/06/03)

Managed Learning Environments Information Pack, JISC series of briefing papers about MLEs, http://www.jisc.ac.uk

Mayer, R.E., Heiser, J. and Lonn, S. (2001) 'Cognitive Constraints on Multimedia Learning: When Presenting More Material Results in Less Understanding', *Journal of Educational Psychology*, 93 (1), pp. 187–98

Microsoft FrontPage, http://www.microsoft.com/frontpage/ (accessed 16/06/03)

Minton, David (1997) *Teaching Skills in Further & Adult Education*, 2nd edn, London: City & Guilds/Macmillan

Moreno, R. and Mayer, R.E. (2000) 'A Coherence Effect in Multimedia Learning: The Case for Minimizing Irrelevant Sounds in the Design of Multimedia Instructional Messages', *Journal of Educational Psychology*, 92 (1): pp. 117–25

Netskills, http://www.netskills.ac.uk/ (accessed 16/06/03)

Paris by the water, http://www.pariswater.com/ (accessed 29/05/03)

Pennie, David, Barnett, Katy, Chin, Paul and Dolphin, Ian (2001) 'From Virtuous to Virtual: The Collaborative Development of Information Skills at the University of Hull', *Vine*, 31 (1), pp. 17–21

PriorITas, PriorITas Links for Interactive Whiteboard Users http://users.argonet.co.uk/users/mhickson/iwb.html (accessed 18/05/03)

Promethean, http://www.promethean.co.uk (accessed 18/05/03)

PsycINFO, http://www.bids.ac.uk (accessed 30/06/03)

Race, Phil and Brown, Sally (1993) *500 Tips for Tutors*, London: Kogan Page

Rada, Roy (1998) 'Efficiency and Effectiveness in Computer-supported Peer-Peer Learning', *Computers in Education*, 30 (3/4), pp. 137–46

RIDING: Gateway to Yorkshire Libraries, http://www.riding.ac.uk/ (accessed 30/06/03)

Rowntree, Derek (1994) *Preparing Materials for Open, Distance and Flexible Learning: An Action Guide for Teachers and Trainers*, London: Kogan Page, in association with the Institute of Educational Technology, Open University

Royal National Institute for the Blind, http://www.rnib.org.uk (accessed 30/06/03)

Rumsby, B. and Middleton, R. (2003) 'Using C&IT to Support Fieldwork on Tenerife', *Planet*, 5 (January), LTSN GEES Publication, available online at http://www.gees.ac.uk/ (accessed 29/05/03)

Selwyn, Neil (1999) 'Virtual Concerns: Restrictions of the Internet as a Learning Environment', Colloquium, *British Journal of Educational Technology*, 30 (1), pp. 69–71

SMART Board, http://www.smartboard.co.uk (accessed 18/05/03)

Smith, M., Hudson, N., Watson, A. and Mackenzie, D. (2002) 'A CD-based Courseware Package for the Teaching and Consolidating of Geological Field Skills', *CAL-laborate*, October (published by UniServe Science in collaboration with the UK Learning and Teaching Support Network, the Swedish Council for the Renewal of Higher Education (formerly known as Council for the Renewal of Undergraduate Education) and BioQUEST Curriculum Consortium, USA, http://science.uniserve.edu.au/pubs/callab/ (accessed 30/06/03)

Stainfield, J., Fisher, P., Ford, B. and Solem, M. (2000) 'International Virtual Field Trips: A New Direction?', *Journal of Geography in Higher Education*, 24 (2), pp. 255–62

Stempleski, Susan and Tomalin, Barry (1990) *Video in Action*, Hemel Hempstead: Prentice Hall

Strolling.com, 'Virtual Tour of Paris', http://www.strolling.com/main/louvre.htm (accessed 29/05/03)

Swailes, Stephen and Senior, Barbara (1999) 'The Dimensionality of Honey and Mumford's Learning Styles Questionnaire', *International Journal of Selection and Assessment*, 7 (1), March, pp. 1–11

TechLearn, Report on Interactive Whiteboards in Education, available online at http://www.techlearn.ac.uk/ (accessed 18/05/03)

Tours of Paris, Webmuseum – Tour of Paris, http://www.ibiblio.org/louvre/paris/ (accessed 29/05/03)

Virtual Reality, Cities of Italy, http://ww2.webcomp.com/virtuale/us/home.htm, Compart Multimedia (accessed 29/05/03)

Voila.fr, French tourist site directly linked to virtual tour, http://tourisme.voila.fr/villes/paris/fra/dec/_vvr/acc.htm (accessed 29/05/03)

Walker, Steve (2003) 'Software Resources for Remedial Physics Teaching in UK University Chemistry Departments', *New Directions in the Teaching of Physical Sciences*, LTSN Physical Sciences Publication, pp. 24–6

Ward, Andy with Baume, David and Baume, Carole (1997) *Assisting with Laboratory Work and Field Trips*, Oxford: The Oxford Centre for Staff and Learning Development

Warr, P., Bird, M. and Rackham, N. (1970) *Evaluation of Management Training* (Chapter 1, 'The CIRO Framework of Evaluation'), London: Gower Press

Web of Knowledge, http://wok.mimas.ac.uk/ (accessed 30/06/03)

Wheeler, John (2003) 'Research Skills for Forensic Science', University of Staffordshire, available online at http://www.physsci.ltsn.ac.uk (listed under workshop reports, Forensic Science Swapshop report workshop 2) (accessed 07/02/04)

Wilkin, Margaret (1995) *Learning to Teach in Higher Education: A Manual of Guidance for Teaching Assistants and Graduate Student Teachers*, Coventry: Centre for Educational Development, Appraisal and Research University of Warwick

Zetoc, http://zetoc.mimas.ac.uk.

Appendix

BOOLEAN OPERATORS

What are Boolean operators?

Boolean operators are based on Boolean logic, invented by George Boole in the 1800s. Boole worked on a system of logic and devised a method of Boolean algebra to organise logical concepts and information into sets. Therefore, Boolean operators allow you to refine searches for information in electronic resources using certain terms so that you find exactly what you are interested in. There is a range of Boolean operators, but the only ones you need to become familiar with for general information searches are listed below. These operators are recognised by most, if not all, commonly available database systems, such as a library catalogue, online journal or subject gateway.

AND

The 'AND' Boolean operator allows you to group together in a single search two or more keywords that represent different concepts to make it more specific:

dyslexia AND education

This will find references on both dyslexia and education as opposed to those on just dyslexia or just education.

NOT

This operator allows you to exclude any non-relevant keywords, such as poverty NOT crime, in order to restrict your search:

canine NOT tooth

This will look for canine but filter out any references to tooth if the search is focusing on the term in relation to dogs, rather than a canine tooth.

OR

Sometimes you may have similar terms or synonyms which you want to search for, such as car OR automobile. The 'OR' Boolean operator will allow you to search for both terms simultaneously and will look for references on either one or the other:

Horse OR equine

References relating to horse or its Greek synonym will be searched for.

Parentheses ( )

Using brackets, or parentheses, allows you to group together similar words or phrases and search for each of them in relation to another different concept:

(vodka OR gin) AND tonic

Here, you will be searching for 'vodka and tonic', and 'gin and tonic'.

Phrases " "

By placing a common phrase in quotation marks it is possible to search for the whole phrase rather than just the individual words:

"nuclear winter"

This search will look specifically for the phrase 'nuclear winter', rather than the words 'nuclear' and 'winter' separately, which could find references of no relevance.

Wildcards *

A wildcard searches for variable characters within a keyword. It allows you to search for words that have variable spellings and to search on a word root. The asterisk (*) is a common wildcard, but some systems use ? or $:

cancer*

The use of a wildcard here will search for 'cancer', 'cancers', 'cancerous' etc., rather than just the single term 'cancer'.

behavi*r

This will search for 'behaviour' or 'behavior'.

Combinations

Using a combination of Boolean operators, it is possible to make quite refined searches that will elicit information very closely matched to your query.

"computer aided design" OR CAD

(mouse OR mice) AND "genetic manipulation"

cancer* AND (lung OR throat) NOT skin

The first two examples are fairly self-explanatory and the third example will search for 'lung cancer' or 'throat cancer' but not 'skin cancer'.

Index